Creative Vegetarian Cooking

"To Live For"

A Collection of Recipes by
Paul Gary

Copyright © 2005
Morris Press Cookbooks

Printed in the U.S.A. by

MORRIS PRESS COOKBOOKS

P.O. Box 2110 • Kearney, NE 68848
800-445-6621 • www.morriscookbooks.com

Introduction

For years people have been asking me how I can survive without eating meat, fish, chicken, eggs, milk and most dairy products (I confess, I do love and still eat pizza with cheese, but I always top it with broccoli, spinach, garlic or other vegetables. I am simply too weak to give up that delicacy)!

Having bought, cooked and eaten great tasting Vegetarian foods for over 10 years and still being alive to talk about it I have decided to put some of my favorite recipes into this book. As you will observe, the recipes are simple, ingredients easy to find and use, and allows for each cook to have flexibility, use creativeness and enjoy making what works best for them.

These are not just Vegetarian recipes, they are healthy, fun and creative recipes for all people who like to cook, create and eat.

I believe in an interactive approach between writer and reader. Measurements can be decided in the making. Whatever brand of food you are comfortable with, use. Be creative, have some fun, add a little more of what you love and a lot less of what you don't. Always look for the freshest ingredients you can find. I love the dried pasta, canned tomatoes, olive oils and balsamic vinegars from Italy, but when it comes to fresh fruits and vegetables I always look for and buy Grown in America produce. You can't get better than that!

I do not use a lot of salt in my recipes but I utilize red pepper flakes, thyme, fresh ground black pepper and fennel quite a bit for seasoning (with lots of garlic, of course). Use the spices you prefer and which work best for you and your taste buds. I happen to like very hot, spicy foods.

Food to me is about eating healthy, being creative, flexible, relaxing and enjoying, with simple techniques and wonderful ingredients that help maximize eye appeal, texture, aroma and of course, taste.

I hope you agree with me and will enjoy the book and my recipes as much as I have enjoyed them over the years. Hopefully you will agree with me that the recipes in the book are *"To Live For"*.

Paul Gary

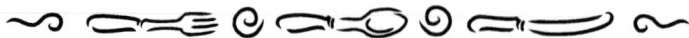

Cooking Essentials

Ingredients "To Live For"

Vegetables
Fresh Broccoli
Fresh Tomatoes
Canned Tomatoes (whole, plum,
    crushed or pureed, from Italy
    if available)
Spinach, fresh or frozen
Russet (Idaho) Baking Potatoes
Fresh White Button Mushrooms
    (underrated, very good
    and inexpensive)
Yellow Onions (underrated
    and inexpensive)
Fresh Red and Green Peppers
Fresh Cauliflower
Fresh Asparagus in season
Fresh Purple Eggplant
Brussels Sprouts (frozen are fine)
Canned Corn
Sweet Potatoes

Beans
Canned Chickpeas
Canned White Beans (whatever
    size the cook likes)

Pasta and Rice
Dried, wide variety of shapes and
    sizes (from Italy if available)
Long grain rice

Tofu and Soy
Extra Firm Low fat Silken Tofu or
    any Tofu desired
Soy Cheese (grated, slices
    and chunks)
Soy "bits" or "crumbles"
Soy Sausages
Tempeh (organic soybeans,
    millet, etc...)

Herbs and Spices
Fresh Garlic (LOTS)
Thyme
Crushed Red Pepper Flakes

Extras
Extra Virgin Olive Oil (from Italy
    if available. Regardless, a
    must item)
Balsamic Vinegar (from Italy
    if available)
Wheat Germ
Egg Substitutes (in refrigerator or
    frozen food section)
Unbleached white or whole
    wheat flour

The Basics for these Recipes

As the compilation of recipes came together to form the chapters and ultimately the cookbook itself, I realized that a few simple, tasty and easy to prepare "basics" actually formed the core to many of the terrific recipes in the book. These "basics" are versatile, easy to prepare and can be refrigerated or frozen for future use. They stand alone or can be used and experimented with to create even more unique dishes.

Use them as little or as much as you prefer. Spice them up; add additional vegetables, beans, or spices as preferred. Try adding leeks or potatoes to the Vegetable broth. Add fresh garlic or additional spices to the pizza dough. The options are endless and experimenting will lead to new, great tasting dishes.

Don't be surprised how simple the "basics" are to prepare. But, when it comes to the tomato sauce and broth, the longer they are simmered the better. Refrigerating them for a day allows the flavors to settle and commingle, the taste becomes even richer.

Spend a few extra minutes and knead the pizza dough a little more than is required to get the feel of it. Add extra olive oil or flour, experiment. Make it thick or thin, the way it works best for you.

My goal is for my readers to eat great tasting, healthy food by participating in the preparation process and taking complete credit for the results. Using the "basics" as needed in this book will surely help to achieve that goal.

Paul Gary

About the Soy and Tofu products in the Book

As you read, try, and enjoy the recipes in my book you will realize that I utilize a lot of different soy or tofu products. Let me mention a few things regarding them. Soy and tofu have become readily available today in not just Health food stores, but in Supermarkets, Deli's, Produce stores, practically anywhere food is sold. There are many popular name Brands to choose from, but by no means are they the only products to buy. I prefer to purchase organic soy or tofu products whenever available (will say as much on the ingredient label). That does not mean the other products are not healthy or good for you, it is strictly my preference. Buy the products or Brands you are comfortable with. Read labels carefully and stay away from any item that has hydrogenated oil in the ingredients, that process might improve taste, but it will not improve your health. The soy or tofu products I incorporate are tasty, pick up the flavors they are cooked with, and are easy to work with and adaptable. Don't be afraid of what you might have heard! Experiment and you will find what works for you. Creativity in cooking is fun and helps to make eating such a wonderful part of our lives.

Relax when cooking and enjoy the experience as much as the result. Try cooking something different because after all, this is food "To Live For".

Paul Gary

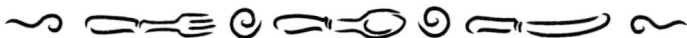

Table of Contents

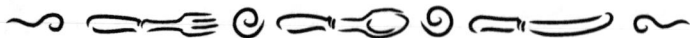

The *B*ASICS RECIPES

THE BASICS RECIPES

BASIC VEGETABLE BROTH

2 lg. yellow onions, diced
5 cloves garlic, diced
2 stalks celery, cut into ¼-inch slices
2 lg. carrots, peeled & cut into ¼-inch pieces
2 heads broccoli, florets & stalks cut in sm. pieces
Extra virgin olive oil
Pinch of red pepper flakes
Pinch of sea salt

Coat the bottom of a large pot with olive oil. Dice the garlic cloves and 1 onion and sauté in the pot until tender, about 5 minutes on high heat. Pour in 4-6 cups of water, adding the second diced onion, celery and the chopped carrots. Bring the water to a boil on high heat, add the salt, red pepper flakes and the chopped up broccoli florets and stalks. Reduce heat to medium, cover and cook for 15 minutes. Reduce to low and simmer for 45 minutes. Strain out the ingredients, leaving only the broth in the pot. Purée the ingredients and pour back into the broth if desired for extra flavor and a thicker texture.

BASIC TOMATO SAUCE

6 lg. tomatoes, quartered or 1 (24-oz.) can whole tomatoes, crushed in saucepan
1 sm. can tomato paste
1 med. yellow onion, diced
5 cloves garlic, diced
Extra virgin olive oil
Pinch of thyme
Pinch of red pepper flakes

Coat the bottom of a medium saucepan with olive oil. Add the diced onion and garlic and sauté over high heat for 5 minutes. Add the fresh tomatoes to the pan or pour in the can of tomatoes, breaking them up. Cook on medium heat for 15 minutes. Reduce the heat to low, stir and then add 3 pinches of thyme and 1 pinch of red pepper flakes. Add 2 tablespoons of the tomato paste to thicken, cover and simmer for 1 hour, occasionally stirring.

BASIC PIZZA DOUGH

1 sm. pkg. yeast
4 c. unbleached white flour
  (100% whole-wheat can be
  substituted)

Sea salt
Warm water
Extra virgin olive oil

In a small bowl add the yeast package, 1 tablespoon of olive oil and 1 cup of very warm water. Stir once, cover with a towel and let sit for 15 minutes. In a large bowl add the flour and salt. Mix together. Pour the warm water and yeast into the flour bowl, stirring slowly with a wooden spoon or with hands until the dough begins to take. Lightly flour a cutting board and knead the dough vigorously for at least 10 minutes into the shape of a ball. Put back in the large bowl and drizzle a small amount of olive oil on top. Cover with a warm, wet towel. Put aside for an hour until dough rises. Knead again for another 10 minutes. When dough is ready it can be used, refrigerated or frozen. A pizza stone is great when baking pizza; it heats from the bottom. Follow the directions, or preheat the oven to 450° and leave the pizza stone in the oven for at least ½ hour prior to baking. Put some cornmeal on a big round with handle wooden pizza tool and transfer the pizza to the tool. Carefully slide the pizza from the wooden tool onto the stone and bake until crisp, 7-8 minutes.

Recipe Favorites

68257A-05

SOUPS

SOUPS

VEGETABLE SOUP

2 lg. yellow onions, diced
½ red pepper, diced
½ green pepper, diced
6 florets cauliflower, sliced in half
8 oz. white button mushrooms, sliced
2 lg. creamer potatoes, cubed, peeled
1 tomato, quartered
8-oz. can chickpeas, drained

1 head broccoli, florets & stalks cut into sm. pieces
6 sm. Brussels sprouts, frozen or fresh (cut in half)
1 lg. carrots, peeled & sliced into ½-inch chunks
6 cloves fresh garlic, cut into chunks
Extra virgin olive oil
Pinch of red pepper flakes

In a large pot add the diced onions, cubed potatoes and sliced carrots. Fill with 8 cups of water, add salt and drizzle in 3-4 tablespoons of extra virgin olive oil. Bring to a boil over high heat. Reduce the heat to medium and cook for 15 minutes. Add the cauliflower, red pepper flakes to taste and Brussels sprouts and continue to cook on medium heat for another 15 minutes. Reduce the heat to low and add the mushrooms, broccoli, red and green peppers, tomato, garlic and chickpeas. Cover and simmer for 1 hour. Stir occasionally. When serving, top with soy Parmesan cheese or wheat germ if desired.

GREEN PEA SOUP

1 (16-oz.) pkg. dried split green
  peas
1 yellow onion, diced
5 cloves garlic
3 lg. carrots, peeled & sliced
  into ½-inch pieces

2 sm. creamer potatoes,
  cubed & peeled
Pinch of red pepper flakes
Extra virgin olive oil
1 c. soy milk or soy cream if
  making into cream soup*

In a pot of salted boiling water (4-5 inches of water) add 2-3 tablespoons of the olive oil, the sliced carrots, diced onion and cubed potatoes. Add a pinch or two of red pepper flakes and boil for 15 minutes on high heat. Pour the package of peas into a colander, wash and drain. Add to the boiling water. Reduce the heat to medium, stir, cover and cook for 45 minutes. Add the whole garlic cloves and simmer on low heat for another ½ hour. Remove from the stove and with a hand held blender, purée the peas and ingredients. A blender can be used as well. Add back to the stove, add a pinch of salt and simmer on low heat for 30 minutes. *If your want to make a cream soup, add the soy milk or soy cream and stir. Stir until smooth and simmer on low heat for 30 minutes.

SPINACH LENTIL SOUP

1-lb. pkg. fresh spinach leaves,
  washed & dried
1 med. yellow onion, diced
2 lg. carrots, peeled & sliced
5 cloves garlic, diced

1 (16-oz.) pkg. dried lentils
Extra virgin olive oil
Pinch of red pepper flakes
Wheat germ
Black pepper

Coat the bottom of a medium-size pan with olive oil. Add the garlic and red pepper flakes and sauté on high heat for 5 minutes. Wash and dry the spinach leaves, leaving the stems on. When dry, add to the garlic and oil and cover the pan. Leave on high heat until the spinach wilts, approximately 3 minutes. Once reduced, stir the oil, garlic and spinach together and then take the pan off the heat. In a large pot add 2 table-spoons of olive oil to 4 inches of water. Boil the water. Dice the onion and carrots and add to the water to cook for 5 minutes. Add the dried lentils and cover, reducing the heat to medium. Cook the lentils for 20 minutes, stirring occasionally. Add the spinach, oil, garlic and pepper mixture to the water and stir in. Reduce the heat to low and simmer for 45 minutes. Check to see that the lentils have loosened up. Stir and continue to simmer for another 15 minutes. Add water if necessary, but soup should be thick and creamy. Using a hand held blender, purée the soup until smooth. Simmer on low heat until ready to serve. Top with wheat germ and grind on black pepper as desired.

68257A-05

CREAM OF BROCCOLI SOUP

3 heads broccoli, florets &
   stems cut up in sm. pieces
1 lg. yellow onion, diced
2 sm. creamer potatoes,
   skinned & cubed
6 cloves fresh garlic, sliced

1 ctn. soy cream or soy milk
Red pepper flakes
Extra virgin olive oil
Sea salt
Wheat germ

In 3 cups of boiling salted water, add 4 tablespoons of olive oil. Add the diced onion and 2 potatoes; cover and cook for 15 minutes on high heat. Reduce the heat to medium and add the broccoli and garlic. Continue to heat for 15 minutes. Remove from the heat and let cool for 5 minutes. With a hand blender, purée the ingredients in the pot, adding a few pinches of red pepper. Simmer on low for 20 minutes. Add ½ cup of soy cream or soy milk, stirring until creamy. Add a pinch or 2 of wheat germ and continue to simmer for 20 minutes.

CREAM OF MUSHROOM POTATO SOUP

Basic Vegetable Broth recipe
   (see recipe), use 4 c.
8 oz. white button mushrooms,
   sliced
3 med. size russet (Idaho)
   potatoes, peeled & diced

1 sm. yellow onion, diced
Wheat germ
Soy cream or soy milk
Sea salt & black pepper

In a pot add the onion to the prepared Basic Vegetable Broth and heat on high for 10 minutes. Reduce the heat to medium and add the potatoes. Cook for 15 minutes and add the sliced mushrooms. Reduce the heat to low, cover and simmer for 20 minutes. Remove from the stove; add 3 tablespoons of wheat germ. Using a hand held blender, purée all the ingredients until smooth. Slowly pour a little of the soy cream or soy milk into the purée while blending until the soup turns a creamy color. Add back to low heat to simmer for 20 minutes, stirring occasionally. Grind on black pepper to taste and serve hot.

PASTA SOUP WITH BRUSSELS SPROUTS

1 lb. pasta shells, sm.
2 med. yellow onions, sliced
1 med. carrot, peeled & cut into
  ¼-inch slices
1 lg. celery stalk, cleaned & cut
  into ½-inch slices

8 oz. frozen or fresh Brussels
  sprouts, sliced in half
Extra virgin olive oil
Red pepper flakes

Add the sliced onions, carrot and celery to a pot with 8 cups of water. Add 4 tablespoons of olive oil and salt. Cook on high heat for ½ hour. Remove from the heat and let cool down for 10 minutes. Strain the liquid broth to remove the vegetables and add the broth back to the pot. Purée the vegetables in a blender with a tablespoon of olive oil and add back to the broth. Bring to a boil on medium-high heat and add the pasta, a pinch or two of red pepper flakes and the sliced Brussels sprouts. Cover and cook for 8-10 minutes. Ladle the soup into bowls and serve hot.

TOMATO AND RICE SOUP

Basic Vegetable Broth (see
  recipe)
1 c. long-grain white rice,
  compare directions on box for
  time

1 lg. yellow onion, diced
4 med. tomatoes, diced
Extra virgin olive oil

In a large pot add 4 cups of the prepared Basic Vegetable Broth from previous recipe. Add the onion and cook on high heat for 15 minutes. Reduce the heat to medium. Add in the rice and stir. Cover and heat for 15 minutes. Reduce the heat to low, add the tomatoes and a drizzle of olive oil, cover and simmer for ½ hour, stirring occasionally. Top with wheat germ as desired and serve hot.

68257A-05

ONION SOUP

Basic Vegetable Broth (see recipe)
6 med. yellow onions, sliced
½ very stale Italian or French bread

Red pepper flakes
Extra virgin olive oil
Soy Parmesan cheese alternative

Prepare the Basic Vegetable Broth per previous recipe. Drain out the vegetables so that only the broth remains or add back for thicker soup. Add 4 cups of the broth to a medium-size pot. Drizzle in some olive oil and a pinch of red pepper flakes. Add the 6 onions. Stir and cook on medium heat for 15 minutes. Reduce the heat to low and simmer for 45 minutes. Cut the stale bread into cubes and add to the broth. Allow simmering for 10 additional minutes. Ladle into soup bowls and generously sprinkle on the soy Parmesan cheese alternative.

Recipe Favorites

Recipe Favorites

68257A-05

SAUCES

SAUCES

CHUNKY TOMATO SAUCE WITH SOY "BITS"

1 pkg. soy crumbles or "bits"
6 lg. tomatoes, diced
1 sm. can tomato paste
1 lg. yellow onion, diced
4 cloves garlic, diced

1 med. green pepper, diced
Extra virgin olive oil
Thyme
Red pepper flakes

Coat the bottom of a large saucepan with olive oil. Add the onion and garlic and sauté for 5 minutes on high heat. Add the package of soy bits, thyme and a pinch of red pepper flakes. Reduce the heat to medium and stir for 8-10 minutes until completely cooked through. Add the diced tomatoes and diced green pepper. Cook for 15 minutes, stirring occasionally. Reduce the heat to low, drizzle in some additional olive oil and stir in the can of tomato paste. Cover and simmer for ½ hour until all the ingredients are blended together. Sauce should be chunky when finished.

SOY SAUSAGE TOMATO SAUCE

1 pkg. soy sausage links
1 (16-oz.) can tomato purée
1 med. yellow onion, diced
6 cloves garlic, diced

4 lg. tomatoes, diced
Dried thyme
Red pepper flakes
Extra virgin olive oil

In a medium saucepan coat the bottom of the pan with the olive oil. Under high heat, sauté the onion and garlic for 5 minutes. Reduce the heat to medium, add the 4 diced tomatoes and stir. Cover and allow cooking for 15 minutes. Reduce the heat to low and add the 16-ounce can or package of tomato purée, the red pepper flakes and a healthy few pinches of thyme. Cover and simmer for ½ hour. Add another pinch of thyme and stir. Break the sausage links in half while still frozen and put them in the sauce. Stir, cover and simmer for 40 minutes on low heat.

WHITE TOFU SAUCE

1 (12- to 15-oz.) pkg. low fat,
  extra firm silken tofu
Extra virgin olive oil

4 cloves garlic, whole
Pinch of red pepper flakes

In a blender add 1 inch of extra virgin olive oil, the tofu (cubed), garlic cloves and a pinch of red pepper flakes. Blend until puréed. Pour into a small pan, cover and simmer for 15 minutes on low heat, stirring occasionally. Use on vegetables, pasta, rice or as a dip.

CREAMY TOMATO SAUCE WITH CHICKPEAS

1 (16-oz.) can tomato purée
1 (12- to 16-oz.) pkg. low fat,
  extra firm silken tofu
3 lg. fresh tomatoes, diced
1 sm. yellow onion, diced
6 cloves garlic, diced
1 red pepper, diced

Thyme
1 (16-oz.) can chickpeas,
  drained
Extra virgin olive oil
Red pepper flakes
Black pepper

In a blender add 1 inch of olive oil and the entire package of tofu, cubed. Pulsate and then purée until smooth. In a large pot coat the bottom with the olive oil. Add the diced onions and garlic and sauté on high heat for 5 minutes. Add the 3 diced fresh tomatoes, 3 pinches of thyme and red pepper flakes (as desired). Reduce the heat to medium and stir for 5 minutes. Add the diced red pepper, stir and then add the 16-ounce can of tomato purée. Reduce the heat to low, cover and cook for ½ hour, stirring occasionally. Pour the tofu into the tomato sauce mixture, stirring until the sauce is smooth and has turned a creamy soft red color. Simmer on low heat for 20 minutes. Add the can of chickpeas and 2 pinches of ground black pepper. Continue to simmer on low heat for another 20 minutes, stirring occasionally. Goes great with pasta. Use as a sauce for pizza or eggplant Parmesan.

68257A-05

CHUNKY VEGETABLE TOMATO SAUCE

1 (16-oz.) can tomato purée	1 lg. onion, diced
4 med. tomatoes, quartered	6 cloves garlic, diced
1 sm. green pepper, diced	Thyme
1 sm. red pepper, diced	Extra virgin olive oil
8 oz. white button mushrooms, sliced	Red pepper flakes

Coat the bottom of a medium saucepan with olive oil. Add the onion and garlic and sauté for 5 minutes on high heat. Reduce the heat to medium and add the quartered tomatoes, stirring until they soften, about 5-7 minutes. Add the red and green peppers and stir for another 5 minutes. Pour in the can of tomato purée and stir all the ingredients together. Add 1 pinch of red pepper flakes and 4-5 pinches of thyme. Stir. Reduce the heat to low, cover and simmer for 30 minutes. Add the sliced mushrooms to the pan. Drizzle on some additional olive oil. Stir, cover and allow simmering for at least 45 minutes.

MUSHROOM TOFU SAUCE

1 (13- to 16-oz.) pkg. extra firm, low fat silken tofu	Black pepper
¼ c. soy milk	8 oz. button mushrooms, cleaned & sliced
3 cloves garlic, whole	

In a blender add the soy milk, whole cloves of garlic and the cubed tofu. Purée until smooth. Add the purée to a saucepan and simmer on low heat for 10 minutes, stirring occasionally. Add the mushrooms, cover and simmer on low heat for 10 additional minutes. Grind on black pepper to taste and serve on pasta, with appetizers or as a dip.

CANNELLINI WHITE BEAN SAUCE

1 (13- to 16-oz.) pkg. low fat,   4 cloves garlic, peeled & left
  extra firm silken tofu   whole
1 (16-oz.) can sm. or lg.   Extra virgin olive oil
  cannellini beans   Red pepper flakes

In a blender add 1½ inches of the olive oil. Add the garlic, 3 pinches of red pepper flakes and pulsate. Add ½ the tofu and ½ the beans. Pulsate then blend until puréed. Add the rest of the tofu and beans and purée until smooth and thick. Pour into a small pan; simmer on low heat for 20 minutes, stirring frequently. Serve warm on pasta, steamed vegetables, as a dip or with rice.

Recipe Favorites

68257A-05

*P*IZZA *and* VEGETABLE PIES

PIZZA AND VEGETABLE PIES

TOMATO AND SOY CHEESE PIZZA

Basic Pizza Dough (see recipe)
Basic Tomato Sauce (see recipe)
1-lb. pkg. shredded soy mozzarella cheese

Pinch of basil
Pinch of oregano
Extra virgin olive oil

Preheat the oven to 375°. Simmer the prepared tomato sauce over low heat. In large 12- to 16-inch pizza pan, drizzle the olive oil on the bottom of the pan and with a paper towel lightly coat the pan. Use a pizza stone if desired; follow stone directions. Knead the prepared basic dough into the bottom of the pan. Put the pan in the oven for 5 minutes to allow the dough to settle and begin to rise. Remove from the oven. Ladle the tomato sauce onto the dough and spread evenly. Sprinkle the shredded soy cheese on the sauce. Drizzle some olive oil on top and add 2 pinches of basil and 1 pinch of oregano. Bake for 20 minutes or until the pie dough browns and the cheese bubbles. Check for sticking by taking a plastic spatula and inserting it under the dough. Spin the pie around so that the spatula covers the entire circumference. Remove from the oven; cut into slices.

VEGETABLE PIZZA

Basic Pizza Dough (see recipe)
Basic Tomato Sauce (see recipe)
2 lg. tomatoes, sliced
½ sm. red pepper, diced
½ sm. green pepper, diced
1 sm. yellow onion, diced
1 (16-oz.) pkg. shredded soy mozzarella cheese
8 oz. white button mushrooms, sliced
Extra virgin olive oil
Red pepper flakes
Thyme

Preheat oven to 375°. In a 12- to 16-inch pizza pan, coat the bottom with olive oil. You can use a pizza stone as well; follow stone directions once the dough is made. Cover the pan completely with the dough. Drizzle a small amount of olive oil on the dough. Ladle a small amount of the premade Basic Tomato Sauce on the dough covering the inside but ending 1 inch from the edge. Slice up a tomato and feather it on the dough. Sprinkle on some thyme and crushed red pepper. Put in the preheated oven for 5 minutes until the dough begins to bake. Remove and sprinkle on the cheese. Add the diced peppers, onions and sliced mushrooms to the top of the cheese. Drizzle a small amount of olive oil on the vegetables. Put back in the oven for 15 minutes until the dough browns but doesn't quite over harden. Run a spatula underneath the pie to check for any sticking.

WHITE POTATO AND ONION PIZZA

Basic Pizza Dough (see recipe)
2 russet (Idaho) baking potatoes, peeled & sliced thin
1 sm. yellow onion, sliced
1 (16-oz.) pkg. shredded soy mozzarella cheese
Pinch of rosemary
Extra virgin olive oil
Black pepper

Preheat oven to 400°. In a 12- to 16-inch pizza pan, lightly oil the bottom. Use a pizza stone if desired and follow the stone directions. Knead the prepared Basic Pizza Dough, adding flour as necessary. Put the dough in the pan and continue to knead. Drizzle a little olive oil on top. Put the sliced potatoes in a microwave for 4 minutes under high heat. Remove and layer on the pizza dough, covering the entire pie. Layer the sliced onion over the potatoes. Sprinkle on additional olive oil and bake in the oven for 5 minutes. Using a spatula, slide it under the pie and rotate to make sure the crust is not sticking to the pan. Remove from the oven, add the soy cheese, top with the rosemary and a little more olive oil and put back in the oven to bake until crispy, about 10 minutes. Grind on black pepper as desired and sprinkle soy mozzarella cheese alternative on top if available.

14

BAKED ZITI PIZZA

Basic Pizza Dough (see recipe)
Basic Tomato Sauce (see recipe)
1 lb. ziti-shaped pasta
1 lb. white button mushrooms, sliced

Dried thyme
1 (16-oz.) pkg. shredded soy mozzarella cheese
Extra virgin olive oil

Preheat oven to 450°. Prepare the tomato sauce in a large pot and let simmer. Add the pasta to boiling, salted water and cook for 7-9 minutes until al dente. Drain and add the pasta to the simmering tomato sauce. Stir until all the pasta is coated. Add a sprinkle of thyme and continue to simmer. Prepare the Basic Pizza Dough according to the recipe. In a large 12- to 16-inch pizza pan, coat the bottom with a thin layer of the olive oil. Knead the dough in the pan, covering the entire bottom and sides. Use a pizza stone if desired and follow the stone directions. Put the pie in the oven and bake for 3 minutes. Take it out and ladle the pasta on top of the dough. Smooth out the ziti evenly on the dough. Top with the cheese and layer the sliced mushrooms over the cheese. Drizzle a little olive oil and a pinch of thyme on top and bake for 15-20 minutes or until the dough turns brown and crusty. Insert a spatula underneath and rotate around the pie to eliminate sticking.

ASPARAGUS AND TOMATO PIZZA

Basic Pizza Dough (see recipe)
1 lb. asparagus, sliced in
¼-inch pieces
2 med. size tomatoes, sliced
thin
8 oz. white button mushrooms,
sliced thin

1-lb. pkg. soy mozzarella cheese
Red pepper flakes
Extra virgin olive oil
Olive oil cooking spray

Preheat oven to 375°. Prepare the dough as per the basic dough recipe. In a large pizza baking tray, spray the bottom of the tray with cooking oil. Knead in the pizza dough to cover the bottom of the pan as well as the sides. A pizza stone can be used in place of the pizza pan. Follow stone directions. Drizzle a little olive oil on the dough and with a paper towel, lightly spread the oil to cover the dough surface. Bake in the oven for 5 minutes and remove. Add the 2 sliced tomatoes to the dough, feathering them on the dough. Cut the asparagus into ¼-inch slices. Steam until they turn color and give off a rich aroma. Drain and add on top of the tomatoes, spreading evenly throughout the pie. Layer the sliced mushrooms on top of the asparagus and tomatoes. Add a pinch of red pepper flakes. Cover with the shredded soy mozzarella cheese, drizzle a little olive oil on the cheese and add back to the oven for 20 minutes or until the dough has browned and turned crusty. Check for sticking by inserting a spatula underneath the dough and rotate around the pan every few minutes.

68257A-05

BROCCOLI AND GARLIC CRUST PIZZA

Basic Pizza Dough (see recipe, use a pizza stone if desired)
Basic Tomato Sauce (see recipe)
6 cloves garlic, diced
2 heads broccoli, florets only
8-oz. pkg. shredded soy mozzarella cheese
Soy Parmesan cheese alternative
Extra virgin olive oil
1 c. unbleached white flour
Black pepper

Preheat oven to 375°. When preparing the Basic Pizza Dough recipe, add the 6 cloves of diced garlic into the flour mixture before allowing the dough to rise. Cover with warm wet towel and allow 1 hour to rise in a dark location. In a 12- to 14-inch pizza pan, drizzle a little olive oil on the bottom. Knead the dough until it covers the entire pan. Tuck in edges. Use a stone if desired and follow directions. Sprinkle some of the unbleached flour on the dough. Put dough in the oven for 3 minutes to begin baking process. Remove and lightly ladle on tomato sauce to cover the dough but leave 1 inch away from the sides of the pan, forming the crust. Sprinkle the soy cheese throughout the dough. Wet the broccoli slightly and put the broccoli florets in a plastic container. Cover with plastic wrap. Microwave on high for 1½ minutes or steam them for 3 minutes. Broccoli should still be firm. Add on top of the cheese. Drizzle on some olive oil and bake for 15-18 minutes until the dough browns. Sprinkle on soy alternative mozzarella cheese and grind on black pepper to taste.

SPINACH CALZONE

Basic Pizza Dough (see recipe)
Sautéed Spinach (see recipe)
8 oz. white button mushrooms, sliced
8 oz. shredded soy mozzarella cheese

Extra virgin olive oil
Pinch of unbleached flour or cornmeal
White Tofu Sauce (see recipe)

Preheat oven to 375°. Use ⅓ the basic dough recipe for this recipe. Flour a baking sheet and knead the prepared basic dough in a circle. A pizza stone can be used as well; follow the stone directions. Spread a thin layer of olive oil on the dough. On ½ of the dough lay the sliced mushrooms; top the mushrooms with the sautéed spinach and garlic and sprinkle with the cheese. Fold the dough over the top and seal using fingers to knead all the edges closed. Add some additional flour or cornmeal to the top of the enclosed dough and bake in the oven for 10 minutes on each side. The White Tofu Sauce recipe in the book can be used in this recipe. Blend the spinach and mushrooms into the sauce. Layer on the dough and fold the dough over, kneading closed the edges. Bake for 10 minutes on each side.

SPINACH AND MUSHROOM QUICHE

Basic Pizza Dough (see recipe)
Sautéed Spinach (see recipe; use 1 lb. in this recipe)
8 oz. white button mushrooms, sliced
1 sm. yellow onion, sliced
1 c. unbleached white flour

1 sm. ctn. Egg Beaters
1 (16-oz.) pkg. soy cheddar cheese, shredded or whole
Pinch of red pepper flakes
Olive oil cooking spray
Wheat germ
Sea salt

Preheat oven to 400°. Spray the insides of a 10-inch aluminum pie pan with cooking spray. Knead the prepared basic dough inside the pan, covering the bottoms and sides. In a large bowl, add the prepared Sautéed Spinach, mushrooms, onion, flour and red pepper. With a wooden spoon mix all the ingredients until covered by the flour. Pour in the Egg Beaters and continue to mix until the Egg Beaters are absorbed. Add a pinch of sea salt. Add ½ the cheese into the mixture and stir vigorously until mixed together. Pour the contents into the pie pan and smooth out evenly. Bake in the oven for 10 minutes without opening the oven door. Remove and sprinkle the remaining 8 ounces of cheese over the top. Sprinkle on 3-4 tablespoons of wheat germ and place back in the oven for another 12-15 minutes until the crust is brown and the cheese has melted through.

68257A-05

TOFU AND VEGETABLE PIE

Basic Pizza Dough (see recipe)
Sautéed Spinach (see recipe; 1 lb.)
8 oz. white button mushrooms, diced
6 T. Egg Beaters
1 (12- to 16-oz.) pkg. low fat, extra firm silken tofu
1 (16-oz.) pkg. shredded soy mozzarella cheese
3 garlic cloves, diced
Unbleached white flour
Olive oil spray
Pinch of red pepper flakes
Sea salt to taste
Wheat germ
Extra virgin olive oil

Preheat oven to 400°. In a large bowl mix the prepared sautéed spinach, tofu, garlic and mushrooms. Add the 6 tablespoons of Egg Beaters, a handful of the flour, a pinch of salt and red pepper flakes and continue to mix until everything is coated. In a 10-inch aluminum pie pan, coat the bottom with the olive oil spay. Knead in the prepared Basic Pizza Dough leaving a thin crust to cover the entire pan and sides. Pour in the mixed ingredients and smooth out evenly in the pie pan. Put in the oven and bake for 5 minutes. Remove and cover with all the shredded cheese. Drizzle a little olive oil over the cheese and sprinkle a handful of wheat germ on top. Put back into the oven and bake for 10-15 minutes until the crust is brown and the ingredients are very hot. Remove, cut into pie slices and serve.

MASHED POTATO PIE

Basic Pizza Dough (see recipe)
Mashed Potato (see recipe)
1 (16-oz.) pkg. shredded soy
  cheddar cheese or 8 soy
  cheddar cheese prepackaged
  slices
8 oz. sliced white button
  mushrooms, sliced

1 (12- to 16-oz.) pkg. soy ground
  "bits" or "crumbles"
1 sm. yellow onion, diced
Extra virgin olive oil
Thyme
Olive oil cooking spray
Sea salt & black pepper to taste

Preheat oven to 400°. In a 10-inch aluminum pie pan, coat the bottom with olive oil cooking spray. Cover the bottom and sides of the pan with the basic dough. Drizzle a thin layer of olive oil on the dough. Ladle in the prepared mashed potatoes, leaving ½ inch from the top of the pan. Add the sliced mushrooms to the top of the mashed potatoes. Add a pinch of salt and pepper as desired. Coat the bottom of a fry pan with olive oil. Add the onion and soy bits. Add 4 pinches of thyme. Sauté on high heat for about 15 minutes. Pour the contents of the pan over the mashed potatoes and smooth out. Bake the pie in the oven for 5 minutes. Take out and layer the entire top of the pie with the cheese. Put back into the oven and bake for another 15 minutes or until the crust begins to brown and the cheese is melted through.

68257A-05

BAKED PASTA AND VEGETABLE PIE

Basic Pizza Dough (see recipe)
12 oz. rigatoni pasta
1 lb. spinach with stems,
  cleaned & patted dry
1 head broccoli, cut into florets
  (discard stalk)

1 lg. tomato, quartered
6 cloves fresh garlic, sliced
8-oz. pkg. shredded soy
  mozzarella cheese
Red pepper flakes
Extra virgin olive oil

Preheat oven to 425°. Add some olive oil to the bottom of a 12-inch aluminum pie pan and spread it evenly with a paper towel. Knead the dough into the pan covering the entire surface. Put the dough into the oven and bake for 4 minutes to initiate the baking process. In a pot of boiling, salted water, cook the rigatoni pasta on high heat for 8-10 minutes until al dente. Drain and add back to the pot. Coat the bottom of a large frying pan with oil. Add in the garlic, broccoli, tomato pieces and red pepper flakes. Sauté on high heat for 5-7 minutes. Add the spinach, reduce the heat to medium and cover the pan. Shake the pan a few times. When the spinach is wilted remove from the heat. Pour the contents of the pan into the pot with the pasta. Stir until all the pasta is coated. Add the package of soy mozzarella cheese to the pot and stir. This recipe does not call for the cheese to be on top of the ingredients in the pie, but mixed in with the ingredients. Add the contents of the pie dough. Drizzle on a little olive oil. Smooth out and bake for 15 minutes until brown and crusty. Cut into pie slices and serve hot, warm or even cold.

SWEET POTATO AND ONION PIE

5 lg. sweet potatoes, peeled &
  cubed
Basic Dough recipe for pizza
  (see recipe)
1 med. yellow onion, diced
Wheat germ

Soy cream or soy milk
Unbleached white flour
Black pepper
Extra virgin olive oil
Sea salt

Preheat oven to 375°. Drizzle a little olive oil into a 10-inch aluminum pie pan and coat with a paper towel. Knead the prepared Basic Pizza Dough into the pan, covering the bottom and sides. Sprinkle a little flour onto the dough. Peel the sweet potatoes and cut them into cubes. Place then in a pot of boiling, salted water for 15 minutes. Drain well and put back into the pot. Add the diced onion. Grind on some black pepper and add a pinch of sea salt. Add a little soy milk or soy cream and using a hand blender, pulsate until the sweet potatoes are mashed and firm, almost lumpy. Do not use too much soy cream or soy milk, the potatoes should not be liquidity. Ladle the sweet potatoes into the pan as a filling for the dough. Grind on additional black pepper to taste and add a handful of wheat germ. Bake for 20 minutes or until the crust has browned and the sweet potatoes are soft and piping hot.

68257A-05

VEGETABLE POT PIE

Basic Pizza Dough (see recipe)
1 (13- to 16-oz.) pkg. low fat,
  extra firm silken tofu
3 cloves garlic, peeled & whole
1 lg. carrot, peeled & cut into
  ½-inch slices
1 sm. turnip, peeled & cubed
1 med. creamer or Idaho potato,
  peeled & cubed
1 sm. onion, diced

8 Brussels sprouts, sliced in
  half
6 white button mushrooms,
  sliced in half
Red pepper flakes
Extra virgin olive oil
Olive oil cooking spray
Unbleached flour
Wheat germ

Preheat oven to 400°. Spray the bottom and sides of 10- to 12-inch aluminum pie pan. Knead the prepared basic dough thinly to cover the surface and sides of the pie pan. Save some of the dough for the covering of the pie. Once the dough has covered the pan, lightly dust with flour. Put in oven for 3 minutes and then remove. In a blender add 1 inch of olive oil, 3 cloves of garlic, a pinch of red pepper and the tofu. Pulsate, then blend until puréed and smooth. Pour into a bowl. Add the diced onion and sliced mushrooms and stir together. Steam the carrot, turnip, potato and Brussels sprouts for 5 minutes. Drain very well and add to the tofu mixture. Stir until all the ingredients are coated. Ladle the ingredients into the pie pan. Smooth out and sprinkle on some wheat germ. Roll out a thin layer of dough, adding a dusting of flour in the process. Cover the pie pan with the dough. Poke a few holes in the dough and drizzle a small bit of olive oil on top. Bake for 20 minutes or until the dough browns.

Recipe Favorites

Recipe Favorites

68257A-05

DIPS, *S*ANDWICHES *and* OMELETS

DIPS, SANDWICHES AND OMELETS

CHICKPEA DIP

1 (16-oz.) can chickpeas,	Extra virgin olive oil
drained	Pinch of crushed red pepper
4 cloves fresh garlic, diced	Pinch of wheat germ

In a blender add 1 inch of olive oil. Add the chickpeas, garlic, red pepper flakes (as desired) and 2 tablespoons of wheat germ. Top with 1 inch of olive oil. Pulsate and blend until smooth, stirring occasionally. Spoon into a container and refrigerate. This makes a great dip or use as a spread for a sandwich or as the starter for baked Chickpea Balls (see recipe).

WHITE BEAN AND RED PEPPER DIP

1 (16-oz.) can white beans,	6 cloves garlic, whole
drained	Red pepper flakes
Extra virgin olive oil	Squeeze of lemon
1/2 med. red pepper, diced	

In a blender, add in 1 inch of olive oil and a squeeze of lemon. Add the white beans, garlic and red pepper. Pulsate then purée. Add 1/3 inch of olive oil and the diced red pepper. Continue to purée. If more liquid is needed, add a little oil.

TWICE COOKED AND MASHED BLACK BEANS DIP

1 (16-oz.) can black beans,	2 cloves garlic, diced
drained	Extra virgin olive oil
1/2 sm. yellow onion, diced	Red pepper flakes

Empty the can of black beans into a bowl and mash with a large fork. In a large frying pan, coat the bottom with olive oil. On high heat, add the mashed black beans. With a spatula, flatten the beans in the pan. Cook for about 7 minutes on both sides. Remove the beans and set aside. Add the red pepper flakes, finely diced onion and garlic into the frying pan. Sauté on high heat for 5 minutes. Add the black beans back into the pan and reduce the heat to medium. Sauté the beans, onion and garlic together for 5 minutes, flip over and continue to sauté for 5 additional minutes or until browned. Serve the beans as a side dish with an omelet, as a dip or sandwich spread.

GRILLED SOY CHEESE AND TOMATO SANDWICH

2 slices whole-wheat bread
1 sm. tomato, sliced thin
4 slices soy cheddar or soy
  mozzarella cheese

Extra virgin olive oil
Sea salt & black pepper to taste

On medium heat, coat the bottom of a frying pan with olive oil. Add 3 slices of the cheese and tomatoes to a slice of bread. Grind on some black pepper and a dash of salt as desired to the tomatoes. Add one slice of cheese on top of the tomato and close the sandwich with the other slice of bread. Press the sandwich down firmly in the hot olive oil using a spatula. After 3-4 minutes (when the bread is good and crusty), flip the sandwich over and press down again. After another 3-4 minutes, flip over one more time for 1 minute. Remove from the heat, cut in half and serve.

SOY SAUSAGE, PEPPERS AND ONION HERO

Soy Sausage Tomato Sauce
  (see recipe)
1 sm. green pepper, sliced
1 sm. red pepper, sliced

1 lg. Italian or French bread
1 (16-oz.) pkg. shredded soy
  mozzarella cheese
Extra virgin olive oil

Preheat oven to 350°. Use the prepared Soy Sausage Tomato Sauce recipe and add the sliced red and green peppers at the same time the sausages are added. Stir all the ingredients together and continue to simmer for 45 minutes as instructed. Slice an Italian or French bread horizontally and lay on a long piece of heavy-duty aluminum foil. Drizzle a little olive oil onto both sides of the bread. Ladle in the sausage, onion, peppers and tomato sauce, covering the bread evenly. Top generously with the shredded soy mozzarella cheese. Bake in the oven for 15-20 minutes until the cheese is melted and the bread is crusty brown. Remove, slice in half and serve.

68257A-05

BROCCOLI AND GARLIC HERO

1 lg. Italian or French bread
2 heads broccoli, florets only
1 tomato, sliced thin
2 garlic cloves, sliced
8 oz. shredded soy cheese,
  mozzarella or cheddar

Extra virgin olive oil
Pinch of red pepper flakes
Sea salt

Preheat oven to 350°. Put the broccoli florets into a microwave container. Add the 2 cloves of sliced garlic. Drizzle on olive oil and add a pinch or 2 of red pepper flakes. Cover in plastic wrap and microwave for 2 minutes. Steamed broccoli can be used as well. Slice a large Italian or French bread horizontally. Drizzle olive oil on both sides. Layer both sides with the tomato slices. Add the broccoli and garlic mixture. Top with the shredded soy cheese and bake for 10-12 minutes until the cheese melts and the bread becomes crispy.

BROCCOLI SLAW HERO

1 lg. Italian or French bread
1 head broccoli, florets & stalks,
  shredded
2 lg. carrots, peeled & shredded
1/2 head fresh green cabbage,
  shredded
1/4 bulb fresh fennel, shredded

1 lg. tomato, sliced thin
1 med. onion, sliced thin
1 jar soy mayonnaise or nonfat
  mayonnaise
Red pepper flakes
Black pepper

In a food processor (if available), finely shred the broccoli, carrots, cabbage and fennel. (You can also buy premade broccoli slaw if available.) Add the ingredients to a bowl with a pinch or 2 of red pepper flakes and mix well with a wooden or plastic spoon. Slice the bread horizontally and lather the mayonnaise onto both insides of the bread, coating completely. Lay the onion slices on one side of the bread and the tomato slices on the other side of the bread. Fill the middle portion of the bread with the broccoli slaw mixture. Grind on black pepper. Close the bread, slice up and serve.

BAKED BREADED TOFU AND TOMATO HERO

Baked and Breaded Tofu (see recipe)
1 lg. Italian or French bread, sliced horizontally
1 lg. tomato, sliced thin
1 sm. yellow onion, sliced thin

8 oz. soy mozzarella cheese in pre-packaged slices
Extra virgin olive oil
Pinch of red pepper flakes
Sea salt

Preheat oven to 350°. Once the baked tofu has been prepared, allow it to cool. Slice a large French or Italian bread horizontally and drizzle olive oil on both sides. Layer the slices of soy cheese evenly on both sides of the bread. Add the sliced tomatoes to the entire length of one of the bread and add a pinch of sea salt as desired. Top with the breaded tofu and add a pinch of red pepper flakes. Layer the slices of onion on top of the tofu. Close the remaining half of the loaf on top and bake for 15 minutes until the bread begins to turn brown and crusty.

CHICKPEA, ONION AND TOMATO SANDWICH

Chickpea Dip (see recipe)
1 med. yellow onion, sliced thin
1 sm. red pepper, sliced thin
1 med. fresh tomato, sliced thin

1 lg. French or Italian bread
Red pepper flakes
Balsamic vinegar

Slice open the bread horizontally and lightly drizzle the balsamic vinegar on the insides of the bread, coating both sides lengthwise. Spread the prepared Chickpea Dip evenly on one side of the bread, coating completely. Sprinkle on some red pepper flakes and layer the onion slices, tomato slices and red pepper slices on top. Close the bread, cut into portions and serve.

68257A-05

SLOPPY SOY JOE SANDWICH

1-lb. pkg. soy "bits" or crumbles
1 sm. onion, diced
2 garlic cloves, diced
1 jalapeño pepper, diced
4 tomatoes, diced
2 pinches of oregano
Balsamic vinegar

1 sm. can tomato paste
Extra virgin olive oil
1 lg. French or Italian bread
8 oz. shredded soy cheddar
 cheese
Black pepper

Preheat oven to 350°. Coat the bottom of a large frying pan with olive oil. Add the onion and garlic and sauté for 5 minutes on high heat. Reduce the heat to medium and add the soy "bits". Sauté for 7 minutes. Add the tomatoes, jalapeño pepper and oregano and cook for 10 minutes until all the ingredients are blended. Drizzle a small amount of balsamic vinegar in the fry pan and stir. With a wooden spoon, add the tomato paste, stir, cover and let cook on low heat for 15 minutes. Place the bread on a large serving plate. Slice the bread open lengthwise and drizzle a small amount of olive oil on both sides of the bread. Generously ladle the Sloppy Soy Joe sauce throughout the insides of the bread, overflowing onto the plate. Top with the shredded soy cheddar cheese. Heat in oven for 2 minutes until cheese melts. Grind on black pepper as desired.

CHICKPEA PITA POCKET

Baked Chickpea Balls (see
 recipe)
1 whole-wheat pita bread, top
 sliced off
½ med. yellow onion, diced
½ med. tomato, diced

6-8 spinach leaves, cleaned &
 left whole
Soy or nonfat mayonnaise
Tabasco sauce
Black pepper

Slice off the top ½ inch of the pita bread. Use a utensil (large fork) and open the belly of the bread carefully so as not to split open the sides. Lightly spread the soy or nonfat mayonnaise on the insides of the pita. Add the spinach leaves to the bottom of the bread. Drop in 4-5 prepared warm Chickpea Balls. Grind on some black pepper. Mix the diced onion and tomato together in a small bowl and then ladle the mixture into the pita. Top with a dash or 2 of Tabasco or hot sauce. Wrap in aluminum foil and heat in the oven under 325° for 2-3 minutes until warm.

BAKED EGGPLANT PARMESAN HERO

Baked Eggplant (see recipe)
Baked Tomato Sauce (see
  recipe)
8-oz. pkg. shredded soy
  mozzarella cheese
4 oz. white button mushrooms,
  sliced

4 cloves garlic, sliced
Extra virgin olive oil
1 lg. Italian or French bread
Soy Parmesan cheese
  alternative

Preheat oven to 350°. Use previous recipes for the Basic Tomato Sauce and the Baked Eggplant. Prepare them both and have ready. Allow the tomato sauce to simmer. The Baked Eggplant can be left warm. Coat the bottom of a small fry pan with olive oil. Add the sliced garlic and mushrooms and sauté for 5-7 minutes until the mushrooms have softened. Sliced open the bread horizontally and drizzle a small amount of oil on both sides of the bread. Ladle the tomato sauce evenly on the bottom side of the bread and layer the baked eggplant slices on top of the sauce. Sprinkle the shredded cheese on top of the eggplant and ladle the mushrooms and garlic on top of the cheese. Freely spoon additional sauce on top of the mushrooms and garlic until the top inside of the bread is coated with sauce and the bread is bursting with ingredients. Wrap the bread in aluminum foil, leaving open the top. Bake for 15 minutes until the bread becomes crusty. Remove from the oven and sprinkle on the soy Parmesan cheese. Cut into slices and serve.

TEMPEH SANDWICH WITH ONIONS AND TOMATO

4-oz. pkg. tempeh, left whole,
  not cubed or crumbled
2 slices 100% whole-wheat
  bread, toasted
1/2 sm. yellow onion, sliced thin

1/2 med. tomato, sliced thin
2 slices soy Swiss, American or
  mozzarella cheese
Black pepper

In a toaster oven bake the tempeh at 400° for 15 minutes. Add the 2 slices of soy cheese to the 2 pieces of wheat bread and toast until lightly brown (darker if desired). Remove from the toaster and put on a plate. Lay the tempeh on one side and add some black pepper. Add the onion and tomato slices on top of the tempeh. Close the sandwich firmly and cut in half. Chickpea dip, chickpea balls (see recipe) or regular chickpeas would make a great side dish with the sandwich.

68257A-05

OMELET WITH SOY CHEESE, SPINACH AND MUSHROOMS

1 lb. fresh spinach, using
  leaves & stems
6 oz. white button mushrooms,
  sliced
2 garlic cloves, diced

1 sm. ctn. Egg Beaters
8 oz. shredded soy cheddar
  cheese
Extra virgin olive oil
Black pepper to taste

In a large frying pan add 6 tablespoons of olive oil and the diced garlic. Sauté on high heat for 3 minutes. Add the diced mushrooms and sauté for 3 minutes. Reduce the heat to medium and add the cleaned and dry spinach leaves and stems. Cover the pan and allow the spinach to wilt down. Remove the cover; stir all the ingredients together. Pour in the container of Egg Beaters, coating the entire pan. Sprinkle on the soy cheddar cheese and put a cover over the pan for 5-7 minutes or until the Egg Beaters is fluffy and there is no remaining liquid. Use a spatula underneath the omelet and rotate around the pan to alleviate any sticking and then flip one half over before serving. Grind on black pepper as desired.

POTATO AND ONION OMELET

1 lg. russet (Idaho) baking
  potato, peeled & diced
1 lg. yellow onion, diced
1/2 green pepper, diced

1 sm. ctn. Egg Beaters
Extra virgin olive oil
Sea salt & black pepper

In a large frying pan coat the bottom lightly with the olive oil. Add the diced onion and potato and sauté on high heat for 10 minutes. Add the diced green pepper, reduce heat to medium and continue stirring for 10 minutes or until the potatoes turn brown and become crispy. Grind in black pepper. Pour in the Egg Beaters, completely coating the shape of the pan and let cook until fluffy. Using a spatula in the underside of the omelet move it around the entire circumference of the pan to prevent sticking. Flip in half and serve. Salt to taste.

BROCCOLI AND SOY CHEESE OMELET

1½ heads broccoli, use florets
  only
3 cloves fresh garlic, sliced
1 (8-oz.) pkg. shredded soy
  mozzarella cheese

1 sm. ctn. Egg Beaters
Extra virgin olive oil
Sea salt & black pepper to taste

Microwave (see previous recipe) or steam the broccoli until tender. In a large fry pan, coat the bottom with olive oil and sauté the garlic for 5 minutes. Add the broccoli to the pan. Reduce the heat to medium and sauté for 5 minutes. Add the Egg Beaters and swirl it around the entire circumference of the pan. Top with the soy cheese and cook until the Egg Beaters are completely fluffy. Using a spatula, go under the omelet and around it completely to prevent sticking. Flip the omelet onto a plate, grind on some black pepper and serve. Salt to taste.

SCRAMBLED EGGS WITH SOY SAUSAGE PATTIES

1 sm. green pepper, diced
1 sm. red pepper, diced
1 sm. onion, diced
2 fresh garlic cloves, diced
1 lg. tomato, sliced
1 sm. ctn. Egg Beaters
4-6 oz. shredded soy cheddar
  cheese

Black pepper
1 pkg. soy breakfast sausage
  patties
Extra virgin olive oil
Olive oil cooking spray

Preheat oven to 425°. Add the 6 soy sausage patties and bake for 20 minutes, turning once until they brown. Remove and put on a large serving platter. In a large fry pan, drizzle a small amount of olive oil to lightly coat the bottom of the pan. On high heat add the onion and garlic and sauté for 3 minutes. Add the red and green peppers and continue to sauté for 3 additional minutes. Reduce the heat to medium and pour in the container of Egg Beaters. Grind on some black pepper and add the shredded soy cheese. Let sit for 1 minute and then with a wooden or plastic spoon fold the mixture until all the liquid has scrambled. Leave on the heat for 1 additional minute to allow the ingredients to settle and the Egg Beaters to fluff up. Remove and add to the serving platter with the sausages. Add tomato slices on the side if desired.

TOFU "HOT DOG" OMELET WITH ONIONS, PEPPERS AND SOY CHEESE

1 sm. ctn. Egg Beaters
2 lg. tofu hot dogs
1 sm. onion, diced
½ sm. green pepper, diced
½ red pepper, diced

4 pre-wrapped slices soy Swiss
 or cheddar cheese
Extra virgin olive oil
Black pepper

Coat the bottom of a large frying pan with olive oil. Slice up the 2 tofu hot dogs into ½-inch slices and add to the pan with the onion, red and green peppers. Sauté on high heat for 5 minutes. Reduce the heat to medium, spread out the onion and peppers evenly in the pan and pour on the Egg Beaters. Lift the pan to coat completely. Let the Egg Beaters settle for 3 minutes. Grind on some black pepper and layer on the soy Swiss or cheddar cheese slices on top of the omelet. Cover the pan and heat for 4-5 minutes until fluffy, eliminating all liquid. With a spatula, carefully go underneath of the omelet to reduce sticking. Fold the omelet in half and flip onto a plate. Add some slices of tomato to the plate for color and flavor.

ASPARAGUS AND TOMATO OMELET

3 asparagus stalks, cut into
 ½-inch slices
2 lg. tomatoes, diced
3 cloves garlic, diced
1 (8-oz.) ctn. Egg Beaters

3 individually wrapped soy
 Swiss cheese slices
Extra virgin olive oil
Black pepper

Steam the asparagus for 5-7 minutes until it becomes soft and fragrant. Drain away any liquid. In a large fry pan, drizzle a small amount of olive oil. Add the garlic and diced tomatoes and stir on medium heat for 5 minutes. Add the asparagus to the pan and stir for 1 minute. Pour in the container of Egg Beaters and swirl around the pan, coating all the edges. Cook for 3 minutes. Swirl again to get any liquid out of the middle of the pan. Use a spatula around the edges of the pan to ensure there is no sticking. Add the 3 slices of soy Swiss cheese to the Egg Beaters and continue to cook for 3-4 minutes until fluffy. Grind on black pepper as desired. Fold the omelet in half in the pan, remove from the heat and flip onto a plate.

TEMPEH OMELET WITH ASPARAGUS AND MUSHROOMS

4 oz. tempeh, cut into cubes
1 sm. ctn. Egg Beaters
6-8 med. white button
  mushrooms, sliced in half
  (stems left on)
6-8 thin asparagus stalks,
  cleaned & cut into ¼-inch
  pieces
4 oz. soy mozzarella cheese,
  diced or shredded

1 lg. garlic clove, quartered or
  sliced
Extra virgin olive oil
Grated soy alternative Parmesan
  cheese
Coarse sea salt for seasoning
  as desired
Black pepper

In a large frying pan (nonstick preferably), coat the bottom with olive oil. Add the cubed tempeh and garlic and sauté for 5 minutes on high heat. Reduce the heat to medium and add the sliced asparagus and mushrooms. Continue to sauté for 5-7 minutes until the asparagus softens. Reduce the heat to medium-low and add the Egg Beaters, swirling it around and through the ingredients in the pan. Add the soy mozzarella cheese; grind or add black pepper and cover the omelet, allowing it to cook for 3-5 minutes. Use a spatula and flip half of the omelet over. Insert the spatula underneath the omelet and turn to ensure no sticking. Allow cooking 2-3 additional minutes. Slide or flip the omelet onto a plate. Sprinkle with soy Parmesan cheese, seasoning with coarse sea salt as desired.

Recipe Favorites

68257A-05

SALADS

SALADS

BROCCOLI SLAW SALAD

1 (12-oz.) pkg. shredded
broccoli slaw (shredded
broccoli, green cabbage &
carrots; can be made just as
easily with same ingredients
using food processor)
8 oz. canned chickpeas, drained
1 sm. yellow onion, sliced

½ red pepper, sliced
6-8 white button mushrooms,
sliced
Pinch of red pepper flakes
Extra virgin olive oil
Balsamic vinegar
Soy mayonnaise (if desired) or
nonfat mayonnaise*

In a large bowl mix the broccoli slaw, chickpeas, red pepper, onion and mushrooms together. Add a pinch of red pepper flakes and stir. Mix 2 parts olive oil to 1 part balsamic vinegar; add, mixing well until all the ingredients are coated with a thin layer of liquid. *In place of the oil and vinegar dressing, a low fat mayonnaise or soy mayonnaise can be used.

TOMATO PASTA SALAD

1 lb. ziti pasta
6 fresh tomatoes, sliced &
quartered
1 red pepper, sliced
1 sm. yellow onion, sliced

1 sm. fennel bulb (if available),
sliced
Extra virgin olive oil
Sea salt

In a pot of salted boiling water cook the pasta over high heat for 7-9 minutes until just right. Drain and pour the pasta into a large bowl, letting cool for 10 minutes. Drizzle red pepper, onion and fennel. Drizzle more olive oil and a pinch of salt and stir vigorously until all the ingredients are coated with the oil. Serve warm or cold.

THREE BEAN VEGETABLE SALAD

8 oz. canned red kidney beans, drained
8 oz. canned cannellini beans, drained
8 oz. canned chickpeas, drained
1 med. yellow onion, diced
6 sm. white button mushrooms, sliced
3 florets raw cauliflower, sliced
4 oz. sugar snap peas in pod (if available)
Balsamic vinegar
Extra virgin olive oil
Red pepper flakes
2 garlic cloves, crushed
Garlicky Bread (see recipe)

In a large bowl add the 3 styles of beans, onion, pepper, mushrooms, cauliflower and snap peas. Toss until mixed together. In a bowl, add 2 parts olive oil to 1 part balsamic vinegar and 2 crushed garlic cloves. Pour over the salad; enough to coat but not drown. Add red pepper flakes to taste. Great with the Garlicky Bread or the Diced Tomato and Garlic Bread.

CORN SALAD

16 oz. canned corn, drained
8 oz. canned chickpeas, drained
6 oz. low fat, extra firm silken tofu, cubed
1 med. yellow onion, diced
½ red pepper, diced
½ green pepper, diced
Balsamic vinegar
Extra virgin olive oil
Red pepper flakes

In a large bowl mix the corn, chickpeas, onion, green and red peppers thoroughly. Cube the tofu. Add to the bowl and stir. Add a pinch of red pepper flakes and stir. In a measuring cup add 2 parts olive oil to 1 part balsamic vinegar. Mix well. Pour over the salad; enough to cover, not drown. Stir until all the vegetables are lightly coated. Serve at room temperature or cold.

68257A-05

MACARONI SALAD

1 lb. elbow macaroni
1 sm. yellow onion, diced
1 sm. red pepper, diced
1 sm. green pepper, diced
1 med. carrots, peeled & diced

1 jar soy mayonnaise or
   substitute nonfat mayonnaise
Red pepper flakes
Black pepper

In a large bowl mix the onion, red pepper, green pepper and carrots. In a pot of boiling salted water cook the elbow macaroni on high for 7-9 minutes until just right. Drain and add back to the pot. Coat with the soy or nonfat mayonnaise. Let the pasta sit until cool. Add the pasta to the bowl of diced vegetables along with a pinch or 2 of red pepper flakes. Stir well until all the ingredients are properly mixed. Cover the bowl with aluminum foil and put in the refrigerator for 1 hour until cool. Grind on black pepper as desired.

SPINACH SALAD WITH TOFU

1 lb. fresh spinach leaves,
   cleaned, patted dry & stems
   removed
2 med. tomatoes, quartered
8 oz. white button mushrooms,
   cleaned & sliced
8 oz. canned chickpeas, drained
1 sm. red pepper, sliced
8 oz. scallions, chopped into
   1/4-inch slices

12 oz. low fat, extra firm tofu,
   cubed
Balsamic vinegar
Extra virgin olive oil
Red pepper flakes
Soy Parmesan cheese
   alternative
Wheat germ
Black pepper

In a large serving bowl, layer the spinach leaves on the bottom. In a large mixing bowl, add the tomatoes, mushrooms, chickpeas, red pepper, tofu cubes and scallions. With a wooden spoon mix them together. In a cup add 2 parts olive oil to one part balsamic vinegar and a pinch or 2 of red pepper flakes. Mix and then slowly drizzle over the mixed vegetables, coating them. Add the ingredients to the serving bowl with the spinach. Sprinkle on the soy Parmesan cheese alternative, grind on black pepper and top with a handful of wheat germ as desired.

TEMPEH AND SPINACH SALAD

4-oz. pkg. tempeh, cubed
1 lb. fresh spinach leaves, washed (remove stems if desired)
6 lg. white button mushrooms, cleaned & sliced in half (stems on)
1/2 med. red pepper, sliced
1 sm. yellow onion, sliced or diced as desired
8 oz. canned chickpeas, liquid removed

4-6 broccoli florets, raw & cleaned
3-5 pitted black olives
1 garlic clove, diced
2-4 oz. soy mozzarella cheese, cubed or slices cut in quarters
Pinch of crushed red pepper flakes as desired
Sprinkle of wheat germ

Dressing:

Fat free Thousand Island dressing (bottled) or extra virgin olive oil (2 parts) & balsamic vinegar (1 part)

Add the spinach to a large bowl. Layer on the onion and red pepper. Add the tempeh, broccoli florets, mushrooms and olives. Top with the chickpeas, cheese and garlic. Sprinkle on red pepper flakes as desired and wheat germ. When serving use tongs or a large spoon and fork. Top with favorite dressing or one of the two dressings mentioned as desired.

Recipe Favorites

68257A-05

SIDE DISHES *and* APPETIZERS

SIDE DISHES AND APPETIZERS

SAUTÉED SPINACH

1 (16-oz.) pkg. spinach leaves & stems, cleaned & patted very dry

6 cloves garlic, sliced
Extra virgin olive oil
Pinch of red pepper flakes

In a pan on high heat, cover the bottom with the olive oil. Add the sliced garlic and red pepper flakes and sauté until the garlic is golden brown. Reduce the heat to medium and add the whole package of spinach. Cover the pan. As the spinach wilts, stir the ingredients together. Remove from the heat and serve using tongs or a perforated spoon to scoop out. Leave excess liquid in pan. Salt to taste.

SAUTÉED BROCCOLI, SPINACH AND CHICKPEAS

1-lb. pkg. fresh spinach, cleaned with stems left on (let dry)
1 head broccoli, florets only
8 oz. canned chickpeas, drained well

6 cloves garlic, peeled & sliced
Red pepper flakes
Extra virgin olive oil

Coat the bottom of a saucepan with olive oil. On high heat add the garlic, 2 pinches of red pepper flakes and chickpeas. Sauté for 5 minutes. Reduce the heat to medium and add the broccoli. Stir, cover and cook for 5 minutes. Make sure that the spinach has been thoroughly dried before adding to the pan. Open the cover and add the spinach to the pan. Stir, then close the cover and continue to cook the spinach until it wilts, about 4 minutes. When the spinach has wilted down remove from the heat. Use tongs or a perforated spoon to put the spinach, broccoli, chickpeas and garlic onto a plate. Discard excess oil. Salt as desired. Use as a side dish or appetizer.

MICROWAVE BROCCOLI

1 head broccoli, florets only	Fresh garlic
Extra virgin olive oil	Pinch of red pepper flakes

In a microwave container add the broccoli and fill the container to the top with water. Empty the water but leave the broccoli wet in the container. Slice up as much garlic as desired (3-4 cloves) and add to the broccoli in the container. Add a small amount of olive oil and a pinch of red pepper flakes. Tightly cover with plastic wrap and microwave on high for 2½ minutes or 3 minutes if preferred softer. Season with salt as desired.

BAKED BROCCOLI BALLS

1 head broccoli, florets only	Crushed red pepper flakes
1 sm. ctn. Egg Beaters	Olive oil spray
Tabasco sauce	Black pepper
Wheat germ	

Preheat the oven to 400°. Cut up the broccoli to use only the florets. Pour the Egg Beaters into a bowl and add a few drops of Tabasco if desired. In a second bowl add 3-4 inches of wheat germ with a few pinches of red pepper flakes and mix. Dip the florets into the wheat germ then the Egg Beaters and then back into the wheat germ. Once coated, lay them on a baking pan that has been coated with an olive oil spray. Lightly spray the florets with the olive oil spray and bake for 10 minutes; turn and bake another 10 minutes until firm and crispy. Grind on black pepper as desired. Can be served hot or cold, as an appetizer, snack or side dish.

FRENCH FRIES & SWEET POTATO FRIES

3 russet (Idaho) baking potatoes & 3 sweet potatoes, skins left on both as desired	Olive oil cooking spray of olive oil
	Salt to taste

Preheat oven to 475°. Slice off the ends of both the potatoes and sweet potatoes. Cut the potatoes on the sides to square off all four sides, making it easier to cut in even horizontal shapes. The size of the fries is up to the cook. Spray a baking sheet with olive oil spray. Lay both the potatoes and sweet potatoes on the sheet and coat them with the olive oil spray. Bake for approximately ½ hour, turning after 15 minutes or when they brown. Leave in oven longer for further browning and crunchy texture.

     68257A-05

GARLIC MASHED POTATOES

3 lg. russet (Idaho) baking
  potatoes, skins on as desired
5 cloves garlic, diced

1 ctn. soy cream or soy milk
Salt & black pepper

Boil salted water on high heat. Cut the potatoes into cubes, leaving the skins on as desired but slicing off the ends of the potatoes. Boil them until a fork can penetrate easily. Drain and put them back into the pot. Dice up the garlic and add to the pot. Add a little soy cream of soy milk, a pinch of salt, lots of black pepper and either mash the old-fashioned way with a masher or fork or use a hand held blender or purée. Add additional cream or soy milk as needed. Skins maintain the vitamins in the potato but they can be peeled if desired before boiling.

MASHED TURNIPS WITH ONIONS

6 turnips, peeled & cubed
1 sm. yellow onion, diced

Soy cream or soy milk
Sea salt & black pepper

Peel and cut the turnips into cubes. Put them in a pot of salted boiling water and cook on high heat for 20 minutes. Drain and add back to the pan. Add the diced onion, grind in some black pepper to taste and 2 pinches of sea salt. Add a small amount of soy cream or soy milk. Using a hand blender, purée the ingredients until smooth, or mash with a masher or fork for texture. Add additional liquid as desired for smoothness.

BAKED TOFU PATTIES

1 (10 to 16 oz.) serving low fat,
  extra firm silken tofu
1 sm. ctn. Egg Beaters

1 (4- to 6-oz.) bowl wheat germ
Pinch of crushed red pepper
Olive oil cooking spray

Preheat the oven to 350°. Empty the Egg Beaters into a bowl. Stir in the red pepper flakes. In another bowl, pour in the wheat germ, about 2 inches worth. Slice the tofu into 8-10 thick slices. Dip the tofu into the wheat germ, then the batter and then the wheat germ again. Spray the bottom of a baking sheet with the oil spray. Put the tofu slices on the baking sheet and lightly spray them. Bake in oven for 15 minutes until crispy, turn over and bake for another 15 minutes. Serve hot, warm or cold. Great in a sandwich, appetizer or covered with sauce.

BAKED TOFU PARMESAN

Basic Tomato Sauce (see
recipe)
1 (16-oz.) can black beans,
drained
1 lb. sautéed spinach (see
Sautéed Spinach recipe)
13-16 oz. baked tofu (see Baked
Tofu recipe)

1 lb. shredded soy mozzarella
cheese
Extra virgin olive oil
Wheat germ
Soy Parmesan cheese
alternative

Preheat oven to 400°. Prepare the Basic Tomato Sauce and heat on medium until bubbly. Add the can of black beans. Stir, reduce the heat to low and simmer for 30 minutes. Prepare the Baked Tofu patties (about 6-8 patties) and leave on a plate. Prepare the sautéed spinach and drain well to eliminate any liquid. In a medium-sized baking dish drizzle olive oil on the bottom and lightly coat with a paper towel. Ladle in some of the tomato sauce and spread evenly on the bottom of the pan. Add 3 pieces of the baked tofu to the sauce. Top with some of the spinach and even out. Add ½ of the shredded soy mozzarella cheese. Repeat the process, using up the rest of the tofu patties, the spinach and the cheese. Ladle the remainder of the sauce on top of the cheese. Sprinkle some wheat germ on top of the sauce and bake for ½ hour until cooked thoroughly. Sprinkle alternative soy mozzarella cheese on and serve.

BREADED BAKED EGGPLANT

1 lg. purple eggplant, sliced
thick with skin left on
Garlic powder
Onion powder

Wheat germ
2 c. unbleached white flour
Olive oil spray

Preheat the oven to 400°. Cut the eggplant into 10-12 slices with the skin on. Put the slices into a heavily salted bowl of water and let sit for 20 minutes. Remove the eggplant and pat dry. Set up 3 small bowls; one filled with the flour, one with the wheat germ and one with the Egg Beaters. Sprinkle generously the garlic and onion powder into the bowl with wheat germ and stir until mixed. Dip each slice first into the flour, then the Egg Beaters and then the wheat germ. Lay the slices out on a large coated baking pan making sure the eggplant slices do not touch each other. Spray each slice lightly with olive oil spray and bake for 15 minutes, turn over, spray and bake again for 15 minutes or until the eggplant is soft but the coating is crusty.

68257A-05

EGGPLANT PARMESAN

1 lg. purple eggplant, thin slices (skinned)
Basic Tomato Sauce (see recipe)
Sautéed Spinach (see recipe)
1 (16-oz.) pkg. shredded soy mozzarella cheese
1 can black beans, drained
Wheat germ
Extra virgin olive oil
Olive oil cooking spray

Preheat oven to 375°. Warm up approximately 3 inches of the prepared Basic Tomato Sauce in a saucepan. Add the can of drained black beans, stir and let simmer for 15 minutes on low heat. Sauté the spinach per previous recipe (use 1 pound spinach) and put on the side. Peel and slice the eggplant into 12-15 fairly thin slices. Put them in a bowl of heavily salted water and let stand for 20 minutes. Remove them and pat dry. Lay them on a large baking pan and lightly spray with cooking oil spray. Bake for 10 minutes, flip, spray and bake for another 10 minutes. Remove them from the oven. Coat the bottom of a baking dish with olive oil or oil spray. Ladle the tomato sauce; enough to cover the bottom of the dish. Add ½ of the eggplant slices; layer on ½ the spinach; top with ⅓ of the cheese. Repeat the procedure by adding sauce over the cheese, add the remaining eggplant slices, add the remaining spinach, sprinkle on ⅓ of the cheese and layer on the remaining tomato sauce mixture. Top with the remaining cheese and sprinkle on some wheat germ. Drizzle on some olive oil and bake for ½ hour or until piping hot and crusty. Let stand for a few minutes to settle and then serve.

TOFU SOY MEATBALLS

1 (16-oz.) pkg. soy "bits or crumbles"
1 sm. ctn. Egg Beaters
Wheat germ to bind, use as much as needed
Pinch of red pepper flakes (as desired)
Garlic powder (healthy amount)
Olive oil spray
Basic Tomato Sauce (see recipe)

Preheat oven to 375°. In a large bowl combine the ground soy bits, Egg Beaters, wheat germ, red pepper flakes and garlic powder. Roll into 6-8 balls. On a baking sheet, coat the bottom with the spray. Add the meatballs and lightly spray. Bake for 20 minutes, turning after 10 minutes. They will not brown very much. As a second way of cooking, add the soy balls to the prepared Basic Tomato Sauce and simmer on medium-low heat for 45 minutes.

STUFFED PEPPERS

2 lg. red peppers, tops & seeds removed
1 lg. green pepper, top & seeds removed
1 pkg. soy bits or crumbles
1 med. size yellow onion, diced
3 garlic cloves, diced
8 oz. shredded soy mozzarella cheese
Wheat germ
Pinch of red pepper flakes
Extra virgin olive oil
Basic Tomato Sauce (see recipe)

Add 2 inches of the prepared Basic Tomato Sauce to a medium-size saucepan. Use medium heat to warm; reduce heat to low and simmer. Coat the bottom of a frying pan with olive oil. Add the diced onion, diced garlic and red pepper flakes. Sauté over high heat for 5 minutes. Add the soy bits to the pan and sauté on medium heat for 10 minutes. Remove from heat. Slice off the tops of the 2 red and 1 green pepper and remove the seeds. Add 1 tablespoon of the soy bits ingredients inside the peppers, then 1 pinch of soy mozzarella cheese followed by another tablespoon of the soy bits ingredients. Top with more soy mozzarella cheese and sprinkle on the wheat germ. Add the peppers to the tomato sauce and add a tablespoon of sauce on top of the peppers. Cover the saucepan and simmer for 30-40 minutes, or until the peppers have softened. Scoop the peppers onto a plate and top with the remaining sauce.

STUFFED MUSHROOMS

8-oz. pkg. lg. white button mushrooms, stems removed
1 (16-oz.) pkg. soy bits or crumbles
1 sm. onion, diced
2 cloves garlic, diced
Red pepper flakes
Thyme
Extra virgin olive oil
Soy Parmesan cheese alternative

Preheat oven to 375°. Coat the bottom of a large frying pan with olive oil. Add a pinch of red pepper flakes, the onion and garlic and sauté on high heat for 5 minutes. Reduce the heat to medium and add the soy bits and 2 pinches of dried thyme. Stir, cover and cook for 15 minutes. Snap the stems out of the mushrooms. Wash and pat dry. Using a small spoon, add a little bit of the cooked soy bits into each mushroom and lay them out on a baking pan. Drizzle a little olive oil over the mushrooms and bake for 15 minutes. Remove, sprinkle some soy Parmesan cheese on top and serve as an appetizer or side dish.

68257A-05

STUFFED TOMATOES WITH RICE IN GREEN PEPPER TOMATO SAUCE

1 (16-oz.) can tomato purée
4 lg. tomatoes, tops removed
2 lg. green peppers, diced
1 sm. onion, diced
Oregano
1 c. long-grain white rice, follow
directions on box

3 cloves garlic, diced
Red pepper flakes
Extra virgin olive oil
Soy Parmesan cheese
alternative

In 2 cups of boiling salted water add a tablespoon of olive oil and the rice. Cook on high heat for 20 minutes until all the liquid is absorbed. Follow directions on the box. Coat the bottom of a large pan with olive oil. On high heat, sauté the onion and garlic for 5 minutes. Add the green peppers to the pan. Reduce the heat to medium and sauté for 5 additional minutes. Pour in the can of tomato purée and add 3 pinches of oregano and 1 pinch red pepper flakes. Reduce the heat to low, cover and simmer for 30 minutes. Slice the top ½ inch of the tomatoes off. Carefully scoop out the insides of the tomatoes and add them to the simmering sauce. Spoon the rice into the tomatoes, filling them completely. Level off at the top. After the sauce has been simmering for 30 minutes, add the filled tomatoes into the sauce. Cover and simmer for 30 additional minutes. Ladle sauce on a plate and spoon out a tomato on top of the sauce. Then ladle additional sauce on top of the tomato. Sprinkle on some of the soy Parmesan cheese.

TOFU AND VEGETABLE STIR FRY

1 (12- to 16-oz.) pkg. extra firm,
low fat silken tofu, cut into
cubes
8 oz. white button mushrooms,
sliced
½ red pepper, sliced
5 cauliflower florets, sliced in
half

8 Brussels sprouts, sliced in
half
8 broccoli florets, left whole
½ sm. fennel bulb, quartered
6 cloves garlic, sliced
Extra virgin olive oil
Balsamic vinegar
Red pepper flakes

Coat the bottom of a large frying pan with olive oil. On high heat add the sliced garlic, cubed tofu, sliced cauliflower florets, a drizzle of balsamic vinegar and red pepper flakes and sauté for 5-7 minutes. Add the sliced pepper, sliced mushrooms and quartered fennel. Continue to sauté for 5 minutes. Add the broccoli florets, drizzle a little balsamic vinegar on and continue to sauté for 5 more minutes. Pour the ingredients into a serving bowl and serve hot.

STEAMED VEGETABLE MEDLEY

1 head broccoli, florets only
(whole)
6 lg. cauliflower florets, sliced in
half
10 baby Brussels sprouts,
whole

6 sm. red potatoes, whole
Extra virgin olive oil
Pinch of rosemary
Red pepper flakes
Sea salt

In a steamer add the cauliflower, Brussels sprouts and red potatoes.
Bring to a boil and steam for 5 minutes. Add the broccoli florets and
continue to steam for 5-7 minutes until all the ingredients have softened.
Remove and put them in a serving dish. Drizzle some olive oil over
them, a pinch of red pepper flakes and 2 pinches of rosemary. Serve
as a side dish or appetizer.

BAKED POTATO WITH TOFU SAUCE AND BROCCOLI

2 lg. russet (Idaho) baking
potatoes
Tofu White Sauce, heated (see
recipe)
Microwave Broccoli (see recipe)
or simply steam broccoli

Soy Parmesan cheese
alternative
Sea salt
Black pepper and sea salt

Preheat oven to 450°. Clean the potatoes and then using a knife or
fork make 3 small incisions. Bake in a microwave oven on high heat
for 5 minutes. Remove and bake in the oven on a baking tray for 15
minutes until fluffy on the inside and crunchy on the outside. Put the
potatoes on a serving plate. Slice them open horizontally and ladle on
the warm tofu white sauce. Grind on black pepper to taste. Top the
sauce with the broccoli. Sprinkle soy Parmesan cheese on top and
serve. Salt to taste.

68257A-05

BAKED POTATO WITH MUSHROOMS, ONIONS AND SOY CHEESE

1 lg. russet (Idaho) baking potato
1 med. yellow onion, sliced
8 white button mushrooms, sliced

8 oz. shredded soy cheddar cheese
Extra virgin olive oil
Sea salt & black pepper

Preheat the oven to 425°. Stick the tip of a knife or fork into the baking potato 3 times to create small incisions. Put the potato into a microwave and on high heat, cook for 5 minutes. Remove and put on a baking sheet. Bake for 20 minutes or until the insides are fluffy and the outside skin is crunchy. In a small frying pan coat the bottom with olive oil and on high heat sauté the onion for 5 minutes. Add the mushrooms; reduce the heat to medium and stir for 5 additional minutes. Remove the potato from the oven and slice open horizontally. Grind on some black pepper and a salt to taste. Pour the onion and mushrooms over the potato, top with the shredded soy cheddar cheese and put back in the oven for 5-7 minutes until the cheese has completely melted.

SPAGHETTI SQUASH

1 lg. yellow squash, cut in half, seeds removed

Extra virgin olive oil
Salt & black pepper to taste

Preheat oven to 400°. Slice the squash in half lengthwise and remove all the seeds. Drizzle extra virgin olive oil on the bottom of a baking sheet and smooth out with a paper towel. Lay the squash down on the pan, insides facing down. Bake for 1½ hours until the entire squash has completely softened. Scoop out the insides with a large fork. Drizzle a little olive oil on top. Salt and pepper to taste.

BAKED WHEAT GERM PATTIES

8 oz. wheat germ
1 sm. ctn. Egg Beaters
Garlic powder

Onion powder
Red pepper flakes
Olive oil cooking spray

Preheat oven to 400°. In a bowl add the wheat germ, 2 tablespoons of the garlic and onion powder and 3 pinches of red pepper flakes. Mix thoroughly. Pour the Egg Beaters into the bowl and by using hands, mix the ingredients together until they hold in the shape of a patty or meatball (whatever shape is desired). Lay them on a coated baking tray. Lightly spray them with the cooking spray and bake for 15 minutes. Turn them over, coat and bake for another 15 minutes. Remove and serve hot, warm or cool as an appetizer, side dish or snack.

BAKED ONION RINGS

2 med. size yellow onions,
  sliced thick
½ c. unbleached white flour
Wheat germ

Red pepper flakes
1 ctn. Egg Beaters
Olive oil cooking spray

Preheat oven to 375°. Slice the onions into thick slices. Add them into a plastic Ziploc bag and pour in ½ cup of flour. Shake until the onions are thoroughly covered and let sit for 5 minutes. In a small bowl, pour the Egg Beaters and mix with 2-3 pinches of red pepper flakes. In a second bowl, pour the ½ cup wheat germ. Take the onion slices individually and dip first into the Egg Beaters, then into the wheat germ. Lay them on a coated baking sheet and lightly spray the onions with the cooking spray as well. Bake for 10 minutes, flip over and continue to bake for 10 more minutes or until coating is crispy. When they are crunchy on both sides, remove from the oven. Serve hot or warm as an appetizer, side dish or in a sandwich as a topping.

68257A-05

CAULIFLOWER AND POTATO BAKE

2 lg. russet (Idaho) baking
  potatoes, peeled & diced
6 florets cauliflower, washed &
  diced
1 med. yellow onion, diced
4 oz. shredded soy cheddar
  cheese

Black pepper
Red pepper flakes
Extra virgin olive oil
Wheat germ

Preheat oven to 450°. Coat the bottom of a large fry pan with olive oil. Add the onion, potatoes and cauliflower and sauté on high heat for 5 minutes. Lower the heat to medium. Add a pinch of red pepper flakes; sauté for 3 additional minutes. Use a spatula to turn over the ingredients and grind on some black pepper (as desired). Let cook for 3 minutes and then flip over again. Continue the process without adding any more pepper until the onion, potatoes and cauliflower turn brown and crusty. Remove from the heat and ladle into a baking pan. Top with the shredded soy cheddar cheese and sprinkle on wheat germ. Bake for 10-12 minutes.

BAKED TOMATOES WITH SOY MOZZARELLA CHEESE

4 lg. tomatoes, tops sliced off
8 oz. shredded soy mozzarella
  cheese

Sea salt
Extra virgin olive oil
Wheat germ

Preheat oven to 400°. Slice the tops off the tomatoes. Coat the bottom of a baking pan with olive oil. Put the tomatoes into the baking pan. Add a pinch of salt to each and drizzle a little olive oil on the top of each. Bake for 10 minutes. Remove and add the soy mozzarella cheese to the top of the tomatoes. Sprinkle wheat germ on the cheese. Put in the oven and bake until the cheese browns, about 10-12 minutes.

BAKED CHICKPEA BALLS

Chickpea Dip (see recipe)   Extra virgin olive oil
1-2 c. wheat germ   Onion powder
½ c. unbleached white flour   Garlic powder

Coat the bottom of a large fry pan with olive oil and put heat on high. Prepare the Chickpea Dip as per previous recipe. In a bowl add 1 cup of wheat germ, ½ cup of flour and 2 tablespoons each of garlic and onion powder. Mix together. Use a spoon to add the chickpea spread to the mixture. Using hands, roll into a small ball and add to the hot olive oil. Do the same with all the Chickpea Dip until there are 6-10 balls, depending on size. Brown them on all sides and remove. Put on a paper towel to drain. Can be served with a hot sauce, white soy sauce or alone as an appetizer, side dish or in a sandwich.

GARLICKY BREAD

1 lg. French or Italian bread   Pinch of thyme
12 cloves fresh garlic, diced   Soy Parmesan cheese
Extra virgin olive oil   alternative

Preheat oven to 350°. Slice the loaf of French or Italian bread horizontally. Drizzle olive oil onto both sides of the bread. Spread 10 cloves of diced garlic evenly through the loaf. Add a pinch or 2 of thyme. If available, sprinkle the soy Parmesan cheese on both sides of the bread and then close the bread. Lightly coat the entire top of the bread with olive oil and spread the remaining 2 cloves of diced garlic on the oil. Wrap in aluminum foil and bake for 6-8 minutes until the bread is crusty. Slice and serve with soups, pastas or salads. The garlic can be rubbed on the bread as well.

BAKED GARLIC

1 lg. head garlic   Extra virgin olive oil

Preheat oven to 375°. Slice off the top of the garlic bulb, about ¼ inch. Do not peel. Put the garlic bulb on a baking sheet and drizzle olive oil over the top. Bake for 45 minutes to an hour until the garlic has browned and become very soft. Remove from the oven and squeeze the garlic out into a small bowl. Can be used as a spread for bread, eaten with pasta or in mashed potatoes.

DICED TOMATO WITH GARLIC BREAD

Baked Garlic (see recipe)
1 lg. tomato, diced
Extra virgin olive oil

Pinch of oregano
½ Italian or French bread

Preheat oven to 400°. Cut the bread into 4 thick slices and bake for 5 minutes until brown and crispy. Remove and spread the prepared Baked Garlic evenly on the bread. Top with the diced tomato, drizzle some olive oil on the tomatoes and add a pinch of oregano to each slice. Goes great with pasta, as an appetizer or snack. In place of the Baked Garlic, simply rub fresh garlic on to the bread.

Recipe Favorites

Recipe Favorites

68257A-05

Stews, Chili *and* Rice Dishes

STEWS, CHILI AND RICE DISHES

WHITE BEAN AND VEGETABLE BARLEY STEW

Basic Vegetable Broth (see recipe)
12 oz. canned white beans, drained
16 oz. barley, follow directions on box
1 head cauliflower florets, sliced

6 oz. white button mushrooms, sliced
8 oz. frozen peas
3 garlic cloves, cubed
Extra virgin olive oil
Pinch of red pepper flakes
Sea salt

In a pot add 4-5 cups of prepared Basic Vegetable Broth, 3 tablespoons of olive oil and a pinch of salt. Bring to a boil and add the barley. Cover and do not stir. Reduce to medium heat and cook for ½ hour. Add the cauliflower and red pepper flakes, stir, cover and cook for 15 minutes. Reduce the heat to low, add the peas, white beans, mushrooms and garlic and simmer for ½ hour or until the barley softens and absorbs all or most of the liquid. Stir and add a little olive oil. Keep on warm until ready to serve.

SOY SAUSAGE STEW

Extra virgin olive oil
16-oz. can strained tomatoes or tomato purée
1 pkg. soy sausage links
2 lg. tomatoes, quartered
1 med. yellow onion, cubed
½ red pepper, cubed
½ green pepper, cubed

4 mid-size creamer potatoes or 2 lg. russet (Idaho) potatoes, peeled
8-oz. can chickpeas, drained
Pinch of crushed red pepper
Pinch of dried thyme
Soy Parmesan cheese alternative

Coat the bottom of a large saucepan with olive oil. Add and sauté the cubed onion for 5 minutes on high heat. Cut the potatoes into big cubes and sauté with the onion for 5-7 minutes on medium heat. Cut the green and red peppers into big cubes and add to the onions and potatoes. Continue to sauté for another 5 minutes. Add the tomatoes, garlic and the can of strained or puréed tomatoes. Continue to cook on medium heat for 10 minutes. Add crushed red pepper to taste and a pinch or 2 of dried thyme. Reduce the heat to low and add the sausage links. Stir and add the chickpeas. Simmer on low heat for 45 minutes. Top with soy Parmesan cheese if available.

POTATO HASH

1 (16-oz.) pkg. soy "bits" or "crumbles"
1 lg. russet (Idaho) potato, peeled & cubed
1 med. yellow onion, diced
1 sm. green pepper, diced
2 cloves garlic, diced
1 med. tomato, diced
8 oz. canned chickpeas, drained well

4 oz. white button mushrooms, sliced
Thyme
Red pepper flakes
Extra virgin olive oil
Wheat germ
Black pepper

Preheat oven to 400°. Coat the bottom of a large frying pan with extra virgin olive oil. Add the diced onion, garlic and cubed potato and sauté on high heat for 10 minutes. Add the diced green pepper and continue to sauté on medium heat for 5 minutes. Add the soy bits, a large pinch of red pepper (as desired) and 3 pinches of thyme. Continue to sauté on medium heat for 10 minutes. Add the diced tomato, mushrooms and chickpeas. Reduce the heat to low, cover and simmer for 15 minutes, stirring occasionally. Remove from the stove and ladle the ingredients into a baking pan that has been coated with olive oil. Add 2-3 tablespoons of wheat germ on top. Bake for 20 minutes until brown and crusty. Grind on black pepper to taste and serve as a side dish.

68257A-05

MASHED SOY "BITS" WITH POTATOES AND MUSHROOMS

1 (16-oz.) pkg. soy "bits" or
"crumbles"
2 lg. russet (Idaho) potatoes,
cubed with skin left on (as
desired)
1 sm. onion, diced
6 lg. white button mushrooms,
sliced

2 cloves garlic, diced
Soy cream or soy milk
Thyme
Extra virgin olive oil
Black pepper

Cut the potatoes into cubes with the skins on. Put them in a large pot of cold water and let sit for 15 minutes. Add salt and boil on high heat for 12-15 minutes until a fork can go through them. Drain and return back to the pot. Grind on black pepper (as desired). Add a little soy cream or soy milk. With a hand blender pulsate the potatoes until mashed. Use a fork if a hand blender is not available. Add liquid as needed but potatoes should end up mashed but firm. Cover, but leave on the stove on warm heat. In a large frying pan, coat the bottom of the pan with a thin layer of olive oil. Add the diced onion and garlic and sauté for 5 minutes on high heat. Add the soy bits and 3-4 healthy pinches of thyme. Reduce the heat to medium and continue stirring for 10 minutes. Reduce the heat to low and add the sliced mushrooms. Cook for 5-7 minutes until the mushrooms have softened and all the ingredients have blended together. Put the mashed potatoes on a serving plate. Create a hole in the middle of the potatoes and ladle in the soy bits, mushrooms and onion. Grind on additional black pepper. Top with wheat germ or shredded soy cheese if desired.

VEGETARIAN CHILI

1 pkg. soy bits or crumbles
1 can soybeans, drained
1 can white beans, drained
1 can kidney beans, drained
1 onion, diced
6 cloves garlic, sliced
1 red pepper, diced
2 jalapeño peppers, sliced
1 pkg. white button mushrooms, sliced

1 (16-oz.) can diced or whole tomatoes
1 can tomato purée
3 pitted & sliced black olives
Dash of wheat germ
Sprinkle of oregano
Sprinkle of crushed red pepper
Extra virgin olive oil

In a saucepan coat the bottom with olive oil. Sauté the soy bits, onion, 2 sliced jalapeño peppers and garlic on high heat for 10 minutes. Add the can of diced tomatoes and soybeans, stirring until blended together. Continue cooking on medium heat for 5 minutes before adding the can of white beans and can of kidney beans. Add the can of tomato purée, the diced red pepper and stir for 10 minutes. Slice mushrooms; add them with the olives, oregano, crushed red pepper and wheat germ. Stir all the ingredients, cover and let simmer on low for 1 hour.

THREE BEAN CHILI WITH CORN

1 (16-oz.) can black beans, drained
1 (16-oz.) can kidney beans, drained
1 (16-oz.) can chickpeas, drained
4 lg. tomatoes, diced
1 (16-oz.) can whole tomatoes

1 lg. yellow onion, diced
8 fresh garlic cloves, diced
1 lg. green pepper, diced
1 (8-oz.) can corn, drained
Extra virgin olive oil
Red pepper flakes
Cayenne pepper
Black pepper

Coat the bottom of a large saucepan with oil. Add the onion and garlic and sauté on high heat for 5 minutes. Add the green pepper and tomatoes, stir and cook on medium heat for 10 minutes. Add the canned whole tomatoes and with a wooden spoon, break open the whole tomatoes. Add a pinch of red pepper flakes and continue to cook on medium heat for 10 minutes. Add the 3 cans of beans and a pinch or 2 of cayenne pepper. Drizzle a little olive oil in, stir, cover and simmer on low heat for 1/2 hour. Add the can of corn and grind on black pepper. Stir vigorously with a wooden spoon, cover and simmer for an additional 1/2 hour. Add additional crushed red, cayenne or black pepper as desired.

68257A-05

BLACK BEANS WITH BARLEY

12 oz. dried barley from ctn. (see instructions on box)
4 c. Basic Vegetable Broth (see recipe)
1 med. yellow onion, diced
2 med. tomatoes, diced
1 (16-oz.) can black beans, drained
Extra virgin olive oil
Pinch of red pepper flakes

In a medium-size pot add the prepared vegetable broth and bring to a boil. Add the barley and red pepper flakes; cook for 30 minutes or until soft and fluffy. There should be a little liquid left with the barley in the pot, if not, add a mixture of water and olive oil. Remove from heat and cover. In a frying pan, coat the bottom with olive oil and add the onion. Sauté on high heat for 5 minutes. Reduce the heat to medium and add the tomatoes. Sauté for 5 minutes. Add the black beans and drizzle in a little olive oil. Stir and cook for 5-8 minutes until the beans have softened. Remove and pour into the barley, stirring together vigorously. Simmer on low heat for 10 minutes.

SOYBEAN CHILI

1 (16-oz.) can soybeans, drained with gelatin removed
1 (16-oz.) pkg. soy crumbles or soy bits
2 lg. tomatoes, diced
1 sm. red pepper, diced
1 med. yellow onion, diced
4 oz. white button mushrooms, sliced
6 cloves garlic, diced
1 (16-oz.) can tomato purée
Thyme
Red pepper flakes
Extra virgin olive oil

Coat the bottom of a large saucepan with olive oil. Add the garlic, red pepper flakes and onion and sauté on high heat for 5 minutes. Add the package of soy bits or soy crumbles and 3 large pinches of thyme. Reduce the heat to medium and sauté for 10 minutes until the soy bits soften. Add the 2 diced tomatoes to the pan. Stir and then cover the pan and let cook for 5 minutes. Add the diced red pepper and sliced mushrooms to the pan. Stir, cover and cook for 5 minutes. Pour in the container of tomato purée and the soybeans. Stir all the ingredients together. Reduce the heat to low, cover and let simmer for 45 minutes, stirring occasionally.

COUSCOUS WITH GREEN PEAS AND CAULIFLOWER

Basic Vegetable Broth (see
 recipe)
1 (16-oz.) box couscous, follow
 cooking directions
8 oz. frozen green peas
6 med. size cauliflower florets,
 sliced

Extra virgin olive oil
Red pepper flakes
Sea salt
Black pepper

In a medium-size pan add 4 cups of prepared Basic Vegetable Broth and a pinch of red pepper flakes. Bring to a boil on high heat. Add the couscous and reduce the heat to medium. Stir and then cover for 7 minutes or until most of the liquid has been absorbed. Steam the cauliflower florets for 5 minutes. Add the peas to the cauliflower and continue to steam for 2-3 minutes until the cauliflower is soft. Pour the peas and cauliflower into the couscous and continue to cook until all the liquid has been absorbed. Grind on black pepper and add salt as desired.

RICE WITH ASPARAGUS, MUSHROOMS AND RED PEPPER

8 oz. long-grain white rice,
 follow directions on box
1 sm. red pepper, diced
8 oz. white button mushrooms,
 sliced

6 asparagus stalks, cut into
 1/4-inch slices (cut off bottom
 inch of stalk)
Extra virgin olive oil
Sea salt

Preheat oven to 300°. Boil 4 cups of salted water in a cast-iron or porcelain enameled pot on high heat. Add the rice and drizzle in some olive oil. Reduce the heat to medium, stir and cover. Cook for 20 minutes. Reduce the heat to low and add the asparagus, red pepper and mushrooms. Stir, cover and simmer for 15 minutes until the rice has absorbed all or mist of the liquid. Remove from the heat. Put the lid on the pot and put in the oven to warm for 10 minutes. Do not open the door when warming. Be sure to use a potholder when removing from the oven. Season with salt as desired.

 68257A-05

RICE BALLS WITH MUSHROOMS

1-lb. pkg. soy bits or soy
  crumbles
1 sm. onion, diced
1/2 green pepper, diced
1 c. long-grain white rice, follow
  directions on box
2 med. tomatoes, diced
1 (16-oz.) can tomato purée

6 cloves garlic, diced
8 oz. white button mushrooms,
  sliced
Thyme
Extra virgin olive oil
Red pepper flakes
Wheat germ

Coat the bottom of a medium saucepan with olive oil. Add the diced garlic and sauté for 5 minutes on high heat. Reduce the heat to medium and add the tomatoes, stirring for 5 minutes. Pour in the tomato purée and add 3 pinches of thyme and 1 pinch of red pepper flakes. Stir, reduce the heat to low, add the sliced mushrooms and simmer. Add 2 cups of water to a pot. Add salt, drizzle in some olive oil and bring to a boil on high heat. Add the rice; reduce the heat to medium and cover. Stir the rice once or twice. When the rice has absorbed all the liquid and is just right, remove from the heat and add the rice to a large bowl. In a large frying pan coat the bottom with olive oil. Add the diced onions and green pepper and sauté on high heat for 5 minutes. Add the soy crumbles or "bits", reduce the heat to medium and stir together for 15 minutes. Remove from the heat. Add the contents of the frying pan to the bowl with the rice along with 3-4 tablespoons of wheat germ. Stir all the ingredients together and allow cooling for 10-15 minutes. Use hands and form small meatballs and put them in the simmering prepared tomato sauce. Allow simmering to continue for at least 1/2 hour. Serve over pasta, as a side dish or appetizer.

RED KIDNEY BEANS WITH TOFU AND RICE

8 oz. long-grain white rice,
  follow directions on box
1 (16-oz.) can red kidney beans,
  drained
1 (13- to 16-oz.) pkg. low fat,
  extra firm silken tofu, cubed

1 sm. yellow onion, diced
4 cloves garlic, diced
1 sm. red pepper, diced
Red pepper flakes
Extra virgin olive oil
Black pepper

Preheat oven to 375°. In a pot with 4 cups of salted boiling water, drizzle in some olive oil and add the rice. Cover and cook on high heat for 20 minutes until most of the liquid is absorbed. Coat the bottom of a large frying pan with olive oil. Add 2 pinches of red pepper flakes, the diced onion and garlic and sauté for 5 minutes on high heat. Add the cubed tofu and diced red pepper. Reduce the heat to medium and sauté for 10 minutes. Reduce the heat to low and add the can of red kidney beans. Stir, cover and simmer for 10 minutes. Add the rice to the frying pan and stir vigorously until all the ingredients have mixed well. Grind on black pepper. Put the frying pan into the preheated oven for 10 minutes to absorb any remaining liquid and finish cooking. Be careful removing; use a potholder.

BAKED RICE WITH TOMATOES, GARLIC AND ONIONS

1 lb. long-grain white rice,
  follow directions on box
8 lg. tomatoes, quartered
1 sm. can tomato paste
4 cloves garlic, sliced

1 lg. yellow onion, sliced
Thyme
Extra virgin olive oil
Red pepper flakes
Wheat germ

Preheat oven to 400°. Boil the rice per the instructions on the box. When the rice is complete, pour it into a large baking pan and put it on the side. In a large frying pan, coat the bottom with a light layer of extra virgin olive oil. Add the garlic and onion and sauté for 5 minutes on high heat. Reduce the heat to medium and stir in the tomatoes and a pinch of red pepper flakes. Cover and cook for 5 minutes. Reduce the heat to low and add the small can of tomato purée and 3 pinches of thyme. Stir, cover and let simmer for 15 minutes. Pour the ingredients into the baking pan with the rice and stir until mixed well. Drizzle a little bit of olive oil throughout the ingredients. Even out the ingredients in the pan and sprinkle on a handful of wheat germ. Bake for 20 minutes or until crusty. Ladle into bowls and serve piping hot.

68257A-05

Pasta

PASTA

MACARONI AND SOY CHEESE

1 lb. favorite shape dried pasta
(elbow, sm. shells or ziti)
2-3 head broccoli florets
6-8 cloves garlic, sliced
1 pkg. fresh white button
mushrooms, sliced

1 (16-oz.) pkg. shredded soy
cheddar cheese
Extra virgin olive oil
Wheat germ
Olive oil cooking spray

Preheat oven to 350°. Spray a baking pan with cooking spray. Boil salted water and cook pasta for 7-9 minutes on high heat until al dente. Add the broccoli florets to a microwave bowl; add a slight amount of extra virgin olive oil and cover with plastic wrap. Microwave for 2 minutes and pour in the baking pan. Sliced 6-8 cloves of garlic and add to the baking pan. Slice the button mushrooms and add to the baking pan. When the pasta is done, drain and add to the baking pan. Pour some extra virgin olive oil over the ingredients and stir the garlic, pasta, mushrooms and broccoli together. Let sit for a few minutes. Mix in the soy cheddar cheese and stir all ingredients together. Don't leave the cheese just on the top of the macaroni bake. Sprinkle a generous amount of wheat germ on top. Bake for 30-40 minutes until browned and crispy. Grind on black pepper to taste.

VEGETARIAN LASAGNA

1 lb. lasagna noodles
1 (24-oz.) can crushed tomatoes
 or tomato purée
1 sm. can tomato paste
3 med. tomatoes, diced
1 (16-oz.) can black beans,
 drained
6 oz. fresh white button
 mushrooms, cleaned & sliced
2 (12-oz.) pkgs. frozen chopped
 spinach (cook ahead of time;
 eliminate excess water)
1 (12-oz.) pkg. extra firm, low fat
 silken tofu

1 (16-oz.) pkg. shredded soy
 mozzarella cheese
1 pkg. frozen soy sausage links,
 broken in half (no need to
 defrost)
1 handful wheat germ
1 sm. yellow onion, diced
1 sm. red pepper, diced
Thyme
Red pepper flakes
Extra virgin olive oil
6 fresh garlic cloves, sliced

Preheat oven to 400°. Coat the bottom of a large pan with olive oil. Sauté on high heat the 3 cloves of diced garlic and the diced onion for 5 minutes. Add the can of crushed tomatoes, tomatoes, thyme and red pepper flakes. Stir; reduce heat to medium, cover and cook for ½ hour. Add the black beans, stir and then add the sausage links (broken in half). Reduce the heat to low and let simmer for 45 minutes. Add the sliced mushrooms and chopped red pepper. Continue to simmer for 10 minutes. Purée the tofu in a food processor or blender with some olive oil and 2 whole cloves of garlic. In a bowl add the tofu to the cooked spinach. Add a pinch of red pepper flakes. Mix well. In a pot of boiling salted water, cook the lasagna for 10-12 minutes until al dente. Drain well. Begin layering process. Add sauce to the bottom of lasagna pan. Layer in lasagna noodles, cover with sauce and add in the spinach and tofu mixture; top with some soy mozzarella cheese. Add another layer of noodles, top with sauce and layer in lots of the soy mozzarella cheese. Add a final layer of noodles, top with the remaining sauce; layer on the remaining cheese. Sprinkle the wheat germ on the top of the cheese; drizzle olive oil on the top of the wheat germ and bake for 30 minutes until piping hot and crusty.

68257A-05

BAKED RIGATONI WITH MUSHROOMS

Basic Tomato Sauce (see recipe)
8 oz. white button mushrooms, sliced
2 tomatoes, sliced
1 (16-oz.) pkg. shredded soy mozzarella cheese

Extra virgin olive oil
Wheat germ
Olive oil cooking spray
1 (16-oz.) pkg. dried rigatoni pasta

Preheat oven to 400°. Heat the tomato sauce (previous recipe) in a saucepan until hot, then simmer. Cook the rigatoni in a pot of salted, boiling water for 7 minutes until the pasta begins to soften; al dente. Remove and drain. Add the pasta to the saucepan and stir, cover and continue to simmer for 15 minutes. The sauce should cover every piece of pasta, but not drown it. In a baking pan, spray the bottom of the pan with olive oil cooking spray. Pour into the mixture of pasta and sauce and evenly distribute in the pan. Slice the mushrooms and add throughout the dish. Put in the oven and bake for 10 minutes. Remove from the oven and top with the cheese. Slice up the 2 tomatoes and spread out on top of the cheese. Drizzle some olive oil on top of the tomatoes and spread a handful of wheat germ on top of the tomatoes. Bake for 20-25 minutes or until the cheese is sizzling and the pasta has turned brown on the edges. Plate and serve; top with soy Parmesan if available.

PASTA WITH WHITE BEANS AND BROCCOLI

1 lb. ziti-shaped pasta
1 (16-oz.) can white beans, drained
4 cloves fresh garlic, diced
1 sm. yellow onion, diced
1 head broccoli, florets only

Soy Parmesan cheese alternative
Pinch of red pepper flakes
Extra virgin olive oil
Black pepper

In boiling salted water cook the ziti for 8-9 minutes until just right. Drain and return to the pot. Drizzle in some olive oil. Coat the bottom of a frying pan with olive oil. Sauté the garlic, red pepper flakes and onion on high heat for 5 minutes. Reduce the heat to medium, add the white beans, stir and cover for 4-5 minutes. Add the broccoli florets and simmer for 5 minutes on low. Remove from the heat and pour the contents into the pot with the ziti. Stir until the pasta is coated well. Generously sprinkle on soy Parmesan cheese alternative if available. Grind on black pepper as desired.

PASTA WITH SPINACH, MUSHROOMS & CHICKPEAS

1-lb. bag spinach leaves,
cleaned & patted very dry
5 garlic cloves, sliced
8 oz. white button mushrooms,
sliced

8 oz. canned chickpeas, drained
1 lb. dried rigatoni pasta
Pinch of red pepper flakes
Extra virgin olive oil
Black pepper

Boil a pot of salted water and add the pasta for 7-9 minutes until just right and al dente. Drain. Wash spinach leaves, patting completely dry. Coat the bottom of a medium saucepan with olive oil. Slice up the garlic and sauté over high heat for 5 minutes. Add the chickpeas, red pepper flakes and sliced mushrooms. Sauté on medium heat until the mushrooms soften, about 5 minutes. Add the spinach leaves and cover the pan. Once the spinach wilts, remove from the heat. Drain out the excess liquid and add the pasta to the spinach pan, stirring until all the pasta is covered. Simmer on low for 5 minutes. Grind on black pepper as desired.

SPINACH NOODLES WITH TOFU AND VEGETABLES

1 (16-oz.) pkg. dried spinach
noodles
1 (12- to 16-oz.) ctn. extra firm,
low fat silken tofu, cubed
1 red pepper, sliced
1 green pepper, sliced
8 oz. white button mushrooms,
sliced
1 yellow onion, diced

½ head broccoli, florets only
4 oz. canned chickpeas, drained
4 cloves garlic, diced
1 sm. fennel bulb, sliced
Pinch of red pepper flakes
Extra virgin olive oil
Soy Parmesan cheese
alternative
Black pepper

In a pot of salted, boiling water cook the spinach noodles for 7-8 minutes until al dente. Drain well. Coat the bottom of a frying pan with olive oil. Dice the onion and garlic; sauté on high heat for 5 minutes. Cube the tofu and add, stirring frequently for another 5 minutes. Lower the heat to medium and add the peppers and fennel. Toss in a large pinch of red pepper flakes and stir until the peppers and fennel soften. Add the broccoli florets and chickpeas and continue to stir. Reduce the heat to low and add the spinach noodles to the tofu and vegetables. Continue to stir for 5 minutes. Sprinkle on the soy Parmesan cheese alternative and grind on black pepper as desired.

68257A-05

SPAGHETTI WITH CHICKPEAS

1 lb. spaghetti	Extra virgin olive oil
1 (16-oz.) can chickpeas,	Pinch of red pepper flakes
drained	Soy Parmesan cheese
6-8 cloves fresh garlic, sliced	alternative

In a large pot boil salted water. Add the spaghetti and cook for 8-10 minutes until al dente. Drain and add back to the pot. Drizzle a little olive oil over the spaghetti. In a frying pan coat the bottom of the pan with the olive oil. On medium-high heat add the garlic and stir for 3 minutes. Add 1-2 pinches of red pepper flakes with the chickpeas. Cook for 5-7 minutes, stirring every 30 seconds. Remove from the heat and pour over the spaghetti. Toss until all the spaghetti is coated with oil and the chickpeas are mixed in well. Sprinkle with soy Parmesan cheese alternative. Serve hot.

BAKED SHELLS WITH TOFU AND SPINACH

1 lb. lg. pasta shells	Soy Parmesan cheese
White Tofu Sauce (see recipe)	alternative
Sautéed Spinach (see recipe)	Wheat germ
Basic Tomato Sauce (see	Extra virgin olive oil
recipe)	Pinch of red pepper flakes
1-lb. pkg. shredded soy	
mozzarella cheese	

Preheat oven to 375°. Add 2 inches of the prepared Basic Tomato Sauce to a saucepan and simmer on low for 30 minutes, stirring occasionally. Cover and remove from the heat. Put the Sautéed Spinach and prepared White Tofu Sauce together in a bowl and mix thoroughly with a wooden spoon. Add 3 tablespoons of wheat germ and a pinch of red pepper flakes to the mixture. In a pot of boiling salted water add the large shells. Cook for 8-9 minutes until they are al dente or just right. Drain and lay them on a baking pan. Spoon a large helping of the spinach and tofu mixture into each shell. Top each shell with shredded soy mozzarella cheese. Drizzle a little olive oil on top of each shell and bake for 15 minutes. Remove from the pan and put the shells on a plate. Lightly top them with the warmed tomato sauce (don't drown them), sprinkle with soy Parmesan cheese and serve.

LINGUINI WITH BLACK BEAN SAUCE

1 lb. linguini pasta
1 (16-oz.) can black beans,
  drained
1 med. yellow onion, diced
4 cloves garlic, diced
½ green pepper, diced

6 lg. tomatoes, diced
2 T. tomato paste
Red pepper flakes
Thyme
Extra virgin olive oil

Cook the linguini in a large salted pot of boiling water for 7-9 minutes until al dente. Drain and add back to the pot. Drizzle a little olive oil over the linguini and stir with a wooden spoon. Coat the bottom of a saucepan with extra virgin olive oil. Add the onion, green pepper and garlic and sauté on high heat for 5 minutes. Reduce the heat to medium and add the thyme, diced tomatoes and red pepper flakes. Stir, cover and cook for 10 minutes. Add the black beans and the tomato paste, stir, cover and cook for 15 minutes on low heat. Pour the contents over the linguini and stir until the linguini has been coated with the sauce.

BAKED SPINACH SPAGHETTI

1 lb. spinach spaghetti or
  whole-wheat spinach spaghetti
Basic Tomato Sauce (see
  recipe)
1 (8-oz.) pkg. shredded soy
  mozzarella cheese

Extra virgin olive oil
6 cloves fresh garlic, sliced
Wheat germ

Preheat oven to 450°. Once the tomato sauce has been prepared, keep it on low heat to simmer. Boil a pot of salted water and add the spinach spaghetti. Cook for 8-10 minutes until the spaghetti is al dente. Test a sample with a fork. Drain the spaghetti and add back to the pot. Coat the bottom of a large fry pan with olive oil; add the 6 cloves of sliced garlic and sauté on high until the garlic begins to brown. Remove from the heat and add the oil and garlic to the cooked spaghetti. Toss until the spaghetti is completely coated. Pour the spaghetti into a large baking pan and put in the oven to bake for 15 minutes. Take out of the oven and ladle in the tomato sauce. Stir the spaghetti to coat with the sauce. Do not drown the spaghetti in sauce. Put back in the oven and continue to bake for 15 minutes. Remove and sprinkle on the soy mozzarella cheese. Drizzle a little olive oil over the cheese and spread a handful of wheat germ on top of the cheese. Put back in the oven and bake for 20 minutes until the cheese browns and the spaghetti gets very crispy, almost crunchy.

66

SPAGHETTI AND SOY TOFU MEATBALLS

Tofu Soy Meatballs (see recipe)
Basic Tomato Sauce (see
  recipe)
1 lb. spaghetti

1 lb. white button mushrooms,
  sliced
Soy Parmesan cheese
  alternative

Prepare the Basic Tomato Sauce. Warm the sauce and leave on low heat to simmer. Prepare the soy "bits" meatballs using the previous Tofu Meatballs recipe. Add them to the sauce and simmer for 45 minutes until the meatballs are cooked through. They will remain soft. In a large boiling pot of salted water add the spaghetti and cook 7-9 minutes until just right. Drain and return to the pot. Pour the sauce and meatballs in with the spaghetti and with a wooden spoon mix thoroughly. Leave on low heat for a few minutes to allow the spaghetti to finish cooking in the sauce. Ladle into bowls, top with soy Parmesan cheese alternative and serve hot.

TOFU "HOT DOGS" WITH MACARONI AND CHEESE

1 lb. elbow macaroni
1 (16-oz.) pkg. tofu hot dogs
1 (16-oz.) pkg. shredded soy
  cheddar cheese
1 med. size yellow onion, diced

1 sm. green pepper, diced
Ground black pepper
1 sm. ctn. Egg Beaters
Wheat germ

Preheat oven to 400°. In a pot of boiling salted water add the tofu hot dogs for 3 minutes. Remove, cut into ½-inch slices and add to a large baking dish. Add the diced onion and green pepper to the baking dish and stir the ingredients together. In a pot of salted boiling water cook the elbow macaroni over high heat for 8-10 minutes until just right. Drain and add back to the pot. Pour the Egg Beaters on the pasta and mix with a wooden spoon until all the pasta has been lightly coated. Grind some black pepper on the pasta. Add the package of shredded soy cheddar cheese to the pasta and mix well. Scoop the pasta and cheese into the baking dish with the tofu and vegetables. Leave any excess Egg Beaters liquid in the pot and discard. Layer the wheat germ on top and bake for ½ hour or until crusty.

BOW TIE NOODLES WITH GARLIC AND OLIVE OIL

1 lb. bow tie-shaped noodles
8 cloves fresh garlic, sliced
Red pepper flakes

Extra virgin olive oil
Black pepper
Parsley

Coat the bottom of a large fry pan with oil. Add the sliced garlic and 2 pinches of red pepper and sauté on high heat for 5 minutes. In a large pot of boiling salted water add the noodles and cook on high heat for 7-9 minutes until just right. Drain and add the noodles to the pan with the garlic and oil. On low heat stir the noodles and coat with the oil and garlic. Simmer for 5 additional minutes. Grind on black pepper to taste and add some parsley flakes for color.

BAKED ZITI WITH ASPARAGUS

1 lb. ziti-shaped pasta
8 oz. asparagus, cut into ¼-inch
  slices
6 cloves fresh garlic, sliced
8 oz. white button mushrooms,
  sliced
1 med. tomato, sliced thin

1 (8-oz.) pkg. shredded soy
  mozzarella cheese
Extra virgin olive oil
Red pepper flakes
Soy Parmesan cheese
  alternative

Preheat oven to 425°. In a large pot of boiling salted water add the pasta. Cook 8-10 minutes until al dente or just right. Drain and add back to the pot. Coat the bottom of a large fry pan with olive oil. Add the garlic and asparagus and sauté for 5-7 minutes on high heat until the asparagus begins to soften and give off an aroma. Add the mushrooms and 2 pinches of red pepper flakes. Stir for 5 minutes on medium heat. Pour the ingredients into the pasta pot and stir with a wooden spoon until the pasta is completely coated. Pour the ingredients into a large baking pan and spread them out evenly. Top with the shredded soy cheese and layer the thinly sliced tomatoes on top of the cheese. Drizzle a little olive oil over the tomatoes and baked for ½ hour until the pasta has browned and become crunchy. Sprinkle generously with the soy Parmesan alternative cheese if available and serve.

BLACK-EYED PEAS WITH PASTA, SCALLIONS AND TOMATOES

1 lb. elbow or any sm. pasta	6 med. tomatoes, quartered
1 (16-oz.) can of black-eyed peas, drained	3 cloves garlic, sliced
	Red pepper flakes
1 med. batch scallions, chopped	Extra virgin olive oil

In a large pot of boiling salted water add the pasta and cook for 8-10 minutes until just right. Drain and add back to the pot. Add the chopped scallions to the pot and drizzle in some olive oil, mixing thoroughly. Coat the bottom of a medium-size fry pan with olive oil. On high heat sauté the garlic for 5 minutes. Add the sliced tomatoes, reduce the heat to medium and stir for 7-8 minutes until the tomatoes soften. Add the drained can of black-eyed peas and a pinch or 2 of red pepper flakes. Stir for another 5 minutes. Pour the contents of the pan into the pot with the pasta. Stir all the ingredients together and let simmer for 5 minutes on low heat, covered.

BAKED TOFU RIGATONI AND CHEESE

1 lb. rigatoni-shaped pasta	Black pepper
1 head broccoli, florets only	Extra virgin olive oil
8-oz. pkg. shredded soy cheddar cheese	Wheat germ
	Soy Parmesan cheese alternative
1 (13- to 16-oz.) pkg. extra firm, low fat silken tofu	
3 garlic cloves, peeled & left whole	

Preheat oven to 400°. In a pot of boiling salted water cook the pasta on high heat for 8-10 minutes until just right. Add the broccoli florets to the pasta 1 minute before the pasta is finished. Drain and add to a large baking pan. In a blender add 1 inch of olive oil to the bottom of the blender. Cube the tofu and add to the blender with the whole garlic cloves. Grind in some black pepper and purée until smooth. Pour the purée over the pasta and mix until the pasta is completely coated. Add the shredded soy cheddar to the pasta. Mix all the ingredients and smooth them out in the pan. Top with a handful of wheat germ and bake for 20 minutes until brown and crispy. Sprinkle on the soy Parmesan cheese and serve.

ELBOW MACARONI WITH SOY "BITS"

1 lb. elbow macaroni
1 (16-oz.) pkg. soy "crumbles or bits"
1 sm. yellow onion, diced

2 med. tomatoes, diced
Thyme
Extra virgin olive oil

In a pot of boiling salted water cook the macaroni on high heat for 7-9 minutes until just right. Drain and leave in the colander. Coat the bottom of a large pan with olive oil. Add the diced onion, 3 pinches of thyme and soy "bits". Sauté on high heat for 5 minutes. Reduce the heat to medium and add the diced tomatoes. Cover and let cook for 15 minutes, stirring 2-3 times. Reduce the heat to low and pour the macaroni into the pan. Stir vigorously, drizzle on a small amount of olive oil, cover and let simmer for 5-7 minutes.

68257A-05

WHITE LASAGNA WITH SOY "BITS" AND MUSHROOMS

1 lb. lasagna noodles
1 (16-oz.) pkg. low fat, extra firm
  silken tofu
4 garlic cloves, peeled & sliced
1 med. yellow onion, diced
8 oz. white button mushrooms,
  cleaned & sliced
1 (16-oz.) can white cannellini
  beans (sm. or lg.), drained

1 (16-oz.) pkg. soy "bits" or
  "crumbles"
1 (8-oz.) pkg. shredded soy
  mozzarella cheese
Thyme
Red pepper flakes
Extra virgin olive oil
Wheat germ

Preheat oven to 375°. In a large pot of salted boiling water cook the lasagna noodles for 10-12 minutes until al dente. Drain. In a blender add 1 inch of the olive oil, 4 cloves of sliced garlic, a pinch of red pepper flakes and the tofu, cubed. Pulsate and then blend well until puréed. Pour into a small pot and simmer over low heat for 10 minutes. Coat the bottom of a large frying pan with olive oil. Add the diced onion and sauté on high heat for 5 minutes. Add the soy "bits" and 4 pinches of thyme. Reduce the heat to medium and continue to sauté for 10 minutes. Reduce the heat to low and add the sliced mushrooms and white beans. Stir, cover and let simmer for 10-12 minutes. In a large baking pan, coat the bottom with olive oil using a paper towel to spread the oil evenly on the bottom and sides. Add a layer of lasagna noodles to the pan and ladle some of the tofu sauce on top, spreading evenly on the noodles. Layer in the soy bits, mushrooms and beans on top, spread evenly and sprinkle on some of the shredded soy cheese. Add a second layer of noodles and repeat the process using all the shredded cheese, soy "bits", beans and mushroom mixture. Save some of the tofu sauce for the topping. Add a 3rd layer of lasagna noodles and coat with the remaining white tofu sauce. Drizzle some olive oil on top of the sauce and sprinkle with a handful of wheat germ. Bake in the oven for 25-30 minutes until the lasagna begins to brown and get crusty. Remove from the heat and let sit for a few minutes before serving so that the ingredients can settle.

LINGUINI WITH BLACK OLIVES, CAULIFLOWER AND BROCCOLI

1 lb. linguini pasta
16 oz. lg. pitted black olives
  (canned or fresh), sliced in half
1 lg. head broccoli, florets only
6 cauliflower florets, sliced in
  half

3 garlic cloves, diced
Red pepper flakes
Extra virgin olive oil
Soy Parmesan cheese
  alternative

In a large pot of salted boiling water cook the linguini on high heat for 7-9 minutes until just right. Drain and add back to the pot. In a large fry pan, coat the bottom with a thick layer of olive oil. Add the diced garlic and sauté on high heat for 5 minutes. Add the cauliflower and 2 pinches of red pepper flakes. Reduce the heat to medium and sauté for 5 additional minutes. Reduce the heat to low and add the olives and broccoli. Stir, cover and cook for 5-7 minutes until the broccoli becomes tender. Add the linguini to the fry pan and stir vigorously until all the pasta is coated and mixed well. Sprinkle on some soy Parmesan cheese and serve hot.

FETTUCCINI PASTA WITH PEAS AND WALNUTS

1 lb. fettuccini pasta
1 (13- to 16-oz.) pkg. low fat,
  extra firm silken tofu, cubed
4 garlic cloves, peeled & left
  whole
8 oz. frozen peas

1 oz. soy cream or soy milk
2 oz. chopped unsalted walnuts
Black pepper
Extra virgin olive oil
Soy Parmesan cheese
  alternative

In a blender add 1 inch of olive oil, 4 whole garlic cloves and the cubed tofu. Grind in some black pepper (as desired). Pulsate and then purée. Add more oil if needed. Pour into a small pan and warm on low heat. Add a small amount of soy cream or soy milk and stir. Add the peas, stir, cover the pan and leave on low for 20 minutes. In a pot of salted boiling water, cook the fettuccini pasta on high heat for 10-12 minutes until al dente; just right. Drain and return to the pot. Add the sauce with peas to the pot and stir until all the pasta is coated. Ladle the pasta into bowls and sprinkle a handful of walnuts on top of the pasta. Sprinkle on soy Parmesan cheese alternative if available and serve.

68257A-05

SMALL PASTA SHELLS WITH TOMATO SAUCE AND EGGPLANT

1 lb. sm. pasta shells
1 sm. purple eggplant, sliced
  with skin left on
3 med. tomatoes, diced
1 sm. onion, diced

2 garlic cloves, diced
1 sm. can tomato paste
Red pepper flakes
Extra virgin olive oil
Black pepper

Preheat oven to 375°. Put the slices of eggplant on a baking tray and drizzle a little olive oil on them. Bake them for 7 minutes on each side. Remove and cut each slice into quarters. In a medium saucepan, coat the bottom with olive oil. Add the diced onion and garlic and sauté for 5 minutes on high heat. Add the tomatoes, 3 pinches of thyme and 1 pinch of red pepper. Reduce the heat to medium, stir and cook for 15 minutes. Add the can of tomato paste. Simmer on low for 15 minutes. In a pot of boiling salted water, cook the pasta on high heat for 7-9 minutes until al dente. Drain well and pour the pasta back into the pot. Add the quartered eggplant and stir with the pasta. Add the tomato sauce and stir until all the pasta is coated. Grind on black pepper as desired.

Recipe Favorites

Recipe Favorites

68257A-05

DRINKS

DRINKS

OLD-FASHIONED "SOY" EGG CREAM

"Chocolate" soy milk   Seltzer

Mix in a glass ⅔ soy milk to ⅓ seltzer. Stir and drink ice cold.

PEANUT BUTTER "SMOOTHIE"

Peanut butter (use brand that   "Chocolate" soy milk
has only peanuts; no   1 banana
hydrogenated oils or added   Pinch of wheat germ
sugars)   Ice cubes

In a blender add the banana, 2 heaping tablespoons of peanut butter and 1 tablespoon of wheat germ. Pour in the chocolate soy milk and 3 ice cubes. Purée until smooth. The amount of soy milk used will determine if you desire a thin or thick smoothie.

Variation: Strawberries or any other fruits can be added or exchanged.

Recipe Favorites

Recipe Favorites

68257A-05

ALPHABETIZED INDEX of RECIPES

INDEX OF RECIPES

BAKED ONION RINGS	48
BAKED POTATO WITH MUSHROOMS, ONIONS AND SOY CHEESE	47
BAKED POTATO WITH TOFU SAUCE AND BROCCOLI	46
BAKED TOFU PARMESAN	42
BAKED TOFU PATTIES	41
BAKED TOMATOES WITH SOY MOZZARELLA CHEESE	49
BAKED WHEAT GERM PATTIES	48
BREADED BAKED EGGPLANT	42
CAULIFLOWER AND POTATO BAKE	49
DICED TOMATO WITH GARLIC BREAD	51
EGGPLANT PARMESAN	43
FRENCH FRIES & SWEET POTATO FRIES	40
GARLIC MASHED POTATOES	41
GARLICKY BREAD	50
MASHED TURNIPS WITH ONIONS	41
MICROWAVE BROCCOLI	40
SAUTÉED BROCCOLI, SPINACH AND CHICKPEAS	39
SAUTÉED SPINACH	39
SPAGHETTI SQUASH	47
STEAMED VEGETABLE MEDLEY	46
STUFFED MUSHROOMS	44
STUFFED PEPPERS	44
STUFFED TOMATOES WITH RICE IN GREEN PEPPER TOMATO SAUCE	45
TOFU AND VEGETABLE STIR FRY	45
TOFU SOY MEATBALLS	43

STEWS, CHILI AND RICE DISHES

BAKED RICE WITH TOMATOES, GARLIC AND ONIONS	60
BLACK BEANS WITH BARLEY	57
COUSCOUS WITH GREEN PEAS AND CAULIFLOWER	58
MASHED SOY "BITS" WITH POTATOES AND MUSHROOMS	55
POTATO HASH	54
RED KIDNEY BEANS WITH TOFU AND RICE	60
RICE BALLS WITH MUSHROOMS	59
RICE WITH ASPARAGUS, MUSHROOMS AND RED PEPPER	58

SOY SAUSAGE STEW	53
SOYBEAN CHILI	57
THREE BEAN CHILI WITH CORN	56
VEGETARIAN CHILI	56
WHITE BEAN AND VEGETABLE BARLEY STEW	53

PASTA

BAKED RIGATONI WITH MUSHROOMS	63
BAKED SHELLS WITH TOFU AND SPINACH	65
BAKED SPINACH SPAGHETTI	66
BAKED TOFU RIGATONI AND CHEESE	69
BAKED ZITI WITH ASPARAGUS	68
BLACK-EYED PEAS WITH PASTA, SCALLIONS AND TOMATOES	69
BOW TIE NOODLES WITH GARLIC AND OLIVE OIL	68
ELBOW MACARONI WITH SOY "BITS"	70
FETTUCCINI PASTA WITH PEAS AND WALNUTS	72
LINGUINI WITH BLACK BEAN SAUCE	66
LINGUINI WITH BLACK OLIVES, CAULIFLOWER AND BROCCOLI	72
MACARONI AND SOY CHEESE	61
PASTA WITH SPINACH, MUSHROOMS & CHICKPEAS	64
PASTA WITH WHITE BEANS AND BROCCOLI	63
SMALL PASTA SHELLS WITH TOMATO SAUCE AND EGGPLANT	73
SPAGHETTI AND SOY TOFU MEATBALLS	67
SPAGHETTI WITH CHICKPEAS	65
SPINACH NOODLES WITH TOFU AND VEGETABLES	64
TOFU "HOT DOGS" WITH MACARONI AND CHEESE	67
VEGETARIAN LASAGNA	62
WHITE LASAGNA WITH SOY "BITS" AND MUSHROOMS	71

DRINKS

OLD-FASHIONED "SOY" EGG CREAM	75
PEANUT BUTTER "SMOOTHIE"	75

How to Order

Get additional copies of this cookbook by e-mailing the Author, Paul Gary at:

Paulgary18@aol.com

The price for each additional book is $7.00 plus $2.00 for handling and shipping. Thank you and I hope you enjoy the recipes.

Paul Gary

Publish Your Own Cookbook

Morris Press Cookbooks has all the right ingredients to make a really great cookbook. Your group can raise $500–$50,000 or create a cookbook as a lasting keepsake, preserving favorite family recipes.

You supply the recipes & we'll do the rest! ™

3 ways to order our **FREE** Cookbook Kit:
- Call us at **800-445-6621, ext. CB.**
- Visit our web site at **www.morriscookbooks.com.**
- Complete and mail the **postage-paid reply card** below.